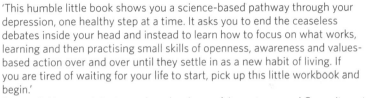

'This humble little book shows you a science-based pathway through your depression, one healthy step at a time. It asks you to end the ceaseless debates inside your head and instead to learn how to focus on what works, learning and then practising small skills of openness, awareness and values-based action over and over until they settle in as a new habit of living. If you are tired of waiting for your life to start, pick up this little workbook and begin.'

Steven C. Hayes, originator and co-developer of Acceptance and Commitment Therapy, Foundation Professor of Psychology, University of Nevada, Reno

Depression affects some 300 million people in the world today and some 1 billion will experience an episode in their lifetime. *The Little Depression Workbook* provides clear evidence-based guidance and practical skills that can help people recover from depression. More than this, it is written with compassion, inspiration and a sense of common humanity; antidotes to the isolation, low motivation and self-doubt that cruelly act as barriers to recovery. Depression is a journey not just out of darkness, but also into the light. This book provides a route map for living life well with and beyond depression.

Willem Kuyken, Ritblat Professor of Mindfulness and Psychological Science, University of Oxford

'A simple and practical guide to overcoming depression through Acceptance and Commitment Therapy. Chock-a-block full of easy-to-use yet surprisingly powerful tools and techniques, this book will help you to break free from the shackles of depression, and build a life worth living.'

Dr Russ Harris, author of *The Happiness Trap and ACT Made Simple*

'*The Little Depression Workbook* is a perfect, user-friendly companion for anyone who is on a path to overcome depression. Bite-sized bits of usable wisdom, coupled with evidence-based practices, can help anyone engaged on a road to recovery.'

Dennis Tirch PhD, author of *The Compassionate Mind Guide to Overcoming Anxiety*

'If you experience depression or low mood, then this book will be a powerful aid on your journey to recovery. Packed full of useful insights and strategies, the authors offer up a solid, evidence-based approach to make big improvements to your life.'

Joe Oliver, founder of *Contextual Consulting* and co-author of *Mindfulness and Acceptance Workbook for Self-Esteem*

'Depression isn't just about feeling sad: it can rob us of motivation, patience, clarity and our sense of purpose. Those make it even harder to start turning things around. *The Little Depression Workbook* offers the perfect approach for this situation: brief as well as thorough, clear as well as evidence-based, purposeful as well as practical & about real change as well as understanding. It goes straight on my "recommended self-help books" list.'

Dr Ray Owen, Consultant Clinical Psychologist, and author of *Facing the Storm* and *Living with the Enemy*

'*The Little Depression Workbook* will help you if you're feeling down, low or hopeless. It is jam-packed with so many practical exercises and relatable accessible cases to help you better understand your depression and the small changes you can make to live a life that feels a lot more fulfilling to you.'

Aisling Leonard-Curtin, C.Psychol., Ps.S.I., Chartered Psychologist, co-director at Act Now Purposeful Living, Peer Reviewed ACT Trainer and co-author of Number 1 Bestseller *The Power of Small*

'This engaging little book provides us with cutting-edge approaches to help those who struggle with depression. Clear and timely, this book will help you understand your challenging emotions and work compassionately with your struggles.'

Russell Kolts, Ph.D. Clinical Psychologist and Professor of Psychology at Eastern Washington University and author of *The Compassionate Mind Approach to Managing Your Anger,* and *Living with an Open Heart*

'Another great entry in the *Little Workbook* series, this book will be useful to anyone wanting to manage the thoughts, feelings and behaviours associated with depression. It is clear and concise, whilst remaining true to the science and principles of contemporary psychotherapy. Its message is much less, "What's wrong with you?", and much more, "What's happening to you?", and it offers loads of practical ideas to the reader.'

Dr Richard Bennett, Clinical Psychologist at Think Psychology, lecturer at the University of Birmingham and co-author of *Acceptance and Commitment Therapy: 100 Key Points and Techniques and The Mindfulness and Acceptance Workbook for Self-esteem*

'Depression is such a painful and lonely experience. Thankfully, this lovely addition to the self-help literature is here to guide and accompany you on your journey to rediscover both fulfilment and connection.'

Dr Mary Welford, Consultant Clinical Psychologist, and author of *Compassion Focused Therapy for Dummies* and *The Kindness Workbook*

'Drs Sinclair and Eisen have created a usable, accessible and compassionate book while staying grounded in science. Through simple but scientifically accurate explanations, relatable examples, and experiential exercises, *The Little Depression Workbook* is a very helpful resource for those suffering from depression.'

Dr Dayna Lee-Baggley, Registered Psychologist in the medical, surgery and cancer care unit at a tertiary level teaching hospital, Assistant Professor in the Faculty of Medicine at Dalhousie University and author of *Healthy Habits Suck*

'Depression is a terrible experience to live through. Gradually, sometimes suddenly, life drains of meaning. The slightest commitment can feel like a mountain to climb. It can feel as if there's no end in sight and it can be hard to see that a meaningful life is still possible, yet it is. In fact, it's because a meaningful life matters so much that we can feel so empty when it loses meaning. This book will show you how to gradually rebuild a meaningful life through the well-validated ACT approach. You'll learn how to distance from your mind's gloomy stories, receive your pain with kindness and nurture, and through meaningful action, build a life worth living. Simple, engaging, effective. This book has all that you need to lift you from depression.'

Benjamin Schoendorff, founder of the Contextual Psychology Institute in Montreal and co-author of the *Essential Guide to the ACT Matrix*

Also available in the Little Workbook series

The Little ACT Workbook

The Little Anxiety Workbook

The Little CBT Workbook

The Little Depression Workbook

The Little Mindfulness Workbook

The Little Self-Esteem Workbook

The Little Stress-Relief Workbook

The Little

Depression

Workbook

Build the life you want with mindfulness, compassion and meaningful action

Dr Michael Sinclair & Dr Michael Eisen

crimson

Important note

The information in this book is not intended as a substitute for medical advice. Neither the authors nor Crimson Publishing can accept any responsibility for any injuries, damages or losses suffered as a result of following the information herein.

The Little Depression Workbook
First published in Great Britain in 2020 by Crimson
An imprint of Hodder and Stoughton
An Hachette UK company

1

Copyright © Dr Michael Sinclair and Dr Michael Eisen, 2020

The right of Dr Michael Sinclair and Dr Michael Eisen to be identified as the authors of this work has been asserted by them in accordance with the Copyright, Designs and Patents Act 1988.

A CIP catalogue record for this title is available from the British Library.

ISBN 978 1 780592 74 9

Printed and bound in Great Britain by Clays Ltd, Elcograf S.p.A.

Hodder & Stoughton policy is to use papers that are natural, renewable and recyclable products and made from wood grown in sustainable forests. The logging and manufacturing processes are expected to conform to the environmental regulations of the country of origin.

Hodder & Stoughton Ltd
Carmelite House
50 Victoria Embankment
London EC4Y 0DZ

www.hodder.co.uk

Contents

About the authors

Dr Michael Sinclair CPsychol AFBPsS CSci is a Consultant
Counselling Psychologist, an Associate Fellow of the British
Psychological Society, a Chartered Scientist registered with the
Science Council, and a Senior Practitioner on the Register of
Psychologists Specialising in Psychotherapy. Following a career
in the NHS, he established City Psychology Group (CPG), a
private therapy practice in the City of London. He currently
serves as the Clinical Director of CPG, offering therapy to
clients using Acceptance and Commitment Therapy (ACT)
and other mindfulness-based approaches, supervision to other
psychologists, ACT coaching to senior executives, workshops for
corporate audiences and the general public, and consultancy to
corporate occupational health departments. Michael has written
seven self-help books including *Mindfulness for Busy People* (now
in its second edition) and *The Little ACT Workbook*, and is regularly
interviewed by the media on topics relating to psychological
wellbeing.

Dr Michael Eisen CPsychol DClinPsy, MA (Cantab) is a Clinical Psychologist with experience in both private practice and the NHS. His private work at City Psychology Group (CPG) is primarily with busy professionals, helping them to overcome depression, anxiety and other common difficulties using mindfulness-based approaches such as Acceptance and Commitment Therapy (ACT). In the NHS, he has worked with clients of all ages, from a wide range of backgrounds, and with the full range of mental health issues, but has specialised in treating violent offenders with serious mental illness. He has a particular interest in mindfulness and meditation, having practised them since 2006, and has undertaken mindfulness teacher training with the Centre for Mindfulness Research and Practice. He has taught mindfulness to NHS staff groups and patients, to corporate groups at Google and other organisations, and to clients in private practice.

Acknowledgments

Thank you to our families, friends and colleagues for their support during the writing of this book, and in particular to Louise Gardner for the wonderful illustrations and Nicole Perkins for her invaluable input. Thank you to all of our clients over the years, for their courage and commitment, without which this book would not have been possible. And finally, thank you to all members of the Association for Contextual Behavioural Science (ACBS), for being a truly inspiring community.

Introduction

Welcome to *The Little Depression Workbook*. We are very pleased that you have decided to read it, but sorry if it is an encounter with depression that has brought you here. Depression is a painful place to be. You might have experienced it before, or this might be the first time. You might wonder whether you even *have* depression. It doesn't matter: we don't need to worry about the exact definition of the word 'depression', or how bad things have to be before we use it. The point is that you are suffering in a way that many other people have also suffered. If you have picked up this book, you might relate to some of the following.

- You have lost your enthusiasm and motivation for things that you used to enjoy.
- You feel bad much of the time, for instance, sad, guilty, ashamed or hopeless.
- You think too much, often about things that have gone wrong for you or could go wrong.
- You feel irritable or get angry easily.
- You criticise yourself and don't like yourself very much.

- You feel lonely, but don't want to see people when you get the chance.
- You have no energy and can't seem to get going.
- Your life feels narrow, empty or unsatisfying.

If any of that sounds like you, then this book can help. You may have tried many ways to escape from depression, or you may feel too worn out to try. You may have come to believe that depression reflects who you truly are, or how the world truly is, or is what you deserve.

We disagree. Depression is not your fault, you are bigger than your depression, and you can do something about it using the principles and skills contained in this book.

Our approach

We are psychologists who have worked with many clients suffering from depression. Our aim here is to offer, in a concise format, the methods that we have found to be most effective, and that are backed up by scientific evidence. So although this workbook may be 'little', its potential impact is not.

We will introduce you to ideas and techniques that are drawn from a group of therapies that take a radical approach to reducing suffering. They are called the *third wave of cognitive and behavioural therapies*, and they make the surprising move of suggesting that it doesn't matter what thoughts and feelings you have, what matters is *how you respond to them*. That might sound strange. You might be struggling with very painful thoughts and feelings and desperately want them to go away. But maybe your efforts to make them go away haven't worked. So maybe it is time to try something different.

The *'third wave'*

The third wave of cognitive and behavioural therapies arose from the meeting of Western psychology and Eastern contemplative traditions from the 1960s onwards. As Western psychologists explored the Eastern traditions, they found that they contained profound insights about the mind and powerful methods for reducing suffering, and they set about integrating them with Western psychological therapies.

In particular, *mindfulness* was adopted, a technique that seeks to relieve suffering not by *changing our thoughts or feelings*, but instead by *changing our relationship with our thoughts and feelings*. Mindfulness means simply noticing thoughts and feelings and letting them be as they are, rather than struggling with them or acting them out. More recently, psychologists have turned their attention to the role of *compassion* in the Eastern traditions, and have integrated compassion for oneself and others into newer third-wave therapies.

In this book, we will be drawing primarily upon ACT (Acceptance and Commitment Therapy), a third-wave therapy developed in the USA by Steven Hayes, Kelly Wilson and Kirk Strosahl. ACT addresses the core processes that keep people stuck in life by using mindfulness and compassion to promote positive behaviour change. As such, ACT can be used in any sitatution, not just with depression. ACT is evidence-based, having been validated (to date) in more than 300 randomised controlled trials, which are the gold standard for research on psychological therapies. Because ACT breaks mindfulness up into several component skills, we won't generally be using the word 'mindfulness' in this book, but instead will cover the skills that comprise it, as they are set out in ACT.

And if you are at all troubled by the spiritual origins of some of the insights and methods offered here – don't be. As you will see, they can be appreciated and used outside of any religious framework and are compatible with any other beliefs that you might hold.

How to use this book

In order to help you free yourself from depression, we will:

- introduce you to relevant psychological theories and principles

- illustrate these with examples from our own clinical work (all case examples are composites, to protect the anonymity of our clients)
- ask you to do brief practical exercises as you read, to help you understand more deeply the ideas being discussed
- teach you exercises that you can do regularly, to help you build the skills that you need.

Practice

Meaningful change happens through *doing*, not just through reading and thinking. Reading this book will be somewhat helpful, but real change will come with doing the exercises and practices included in it. You are working against habits that have built up over a lifetime and instincts that are common to us all, and instead learning new ways of responding to your thoughts and feelings. As with any new skill, this takes practice.

It is not a linear process – once you have read the book and started working on the skills taught in it, you will need to keep working on all of them together. And you need to practise the skills regularly, even when you are feeling fine, rather than turning to them only in a crisis.

Think of learning to play a sport. You would not expect to learn to play football at a high level just by reading about how to do it. And you would not wait until you were on the pitch to try out a new technique that you had read about. You would expect to put in a lot of time practising your skills, so that they are second nature by the time you really need them. You would shoot penalty after penalty, kick cross after cross, slowly honing all the skills of playing football. Eventually you would *just know*, physically, how to kick the ball, without having to think about it too much. The skills offered here can also become something you *just know* how to do. The benefits can begin to show up quite quickly or they can take some time. But either way, they increase the more practice you do.

What works?

There is another radical move that we want you to make. We want you to stop asking, 'Is this true?', and instead ask, 'Does it work?' We can get into endless debates with ourselves and others over what is true, and often it gets us no closer to the life that we want to live. Often our clients who suffer from depression have very strong views about themselves, such as, 'I am a failure'. And if we were to disagree with them, they would prove us wrong a hundred times over, with numerous examples from their lives and other pieces of evidence, and maybe also clever logical arguments. Who can say if they are right or not? Who can define what a 'failure' is, or say for sure whether they are one? What we can say is that calling yourself a failure probably does not help you to live a satisfying life. So, the better question is, 'Does believing this or debating it constantly take me closer to where I want to be?' Or, to put it another way, '*Is this workable?*'

Try it!

The only way to know what will work for you is to try it out. Again, we could get into endless debates about what seems most likely to work. And in doing so, we could probably talk ourselves out of trying most things. So we encourage you to put those debates aside and test things out. Think of yourself as a scientist: they don't just test their theories in debate; they do it in the laboratory, in experiments. So we invite you to test out what we offer you in the laboratory of your own life, and let your experience be your guide as to whether something helps you or not.

Be kind to yourself

If you are suffering from depression, you might be in the habit of speaking harshly to yourself. You might even think it's a good idea, or be so used to doing it that you aren't even aware you're doing it. We will talk about this a lot more in Chapter 6, but for now we want to suggest that you be kind to yourself as you read this book. What do we mean by this? Well, you might find it hard to do all the exercises we suggest, or to practise them consistently, or they might not seem to work for you, or you might find it hard even to read the book. If so, be kind and supportive to yourself, just as you would a friend who was in your situation. Everything is harder when you are experiencing depression, and a kindly approach is always more *workable* than a harsh one. We do better with kindly encouragement than with criticism and contempt.

Beyond this book

While we hope that this book will be helpful, it is not intended to be a comprehensive answer to depression. You might want to seek out other kinds of help, whether after you finish the book, alongside it, or even at this point.

The Little Depression Workbook is an introduction to ideas and methods drawn from therapies that would normally be delivered in person by a therapist. It is not a replacement for in-person therapy. A therapist can work with you in ways that are tailored to your particular circumstances, issues and preferences. And a therapist can form a relationship with you that is warm and supportive: we know from research that a good relationship between therapist and client leads to effective therapy.

There are other self-help books (some of which we've listed on *p179*) that will give you a more detailed introduction to the therapies we draw on here, whereas this book is an effort to integrate their ideas and methods in a compact format. If you find it helpful, you might want to explore a particular therapy further, whether in another book or with a therapist. And this book has not itself been scientifically validated. The research on third-wave therapies mainly looks at face-to-face therapy, rather than self-help books; so, while the ideas and methods presented here have been scientifically tested, this particular presentation of them has not.

And finally, there is nothing that works for everyone, all the time. Different people respond to different therapies, at different times. So, while this book might be just what you need, it also might not suit you right now, and you might find another approach more helpful. The only way to know is to try it and see.

If things are really bad

Unfortunately, it is common for people suffering from depression to think of hurting or even killing themselves, and, sadly, a small proportion of them act on these thoughts. If you are having thoughts of that kind, then we are really sorry that things are so bad.

If you are thinking of harming yourself, then we recommend that you seek some extra support alongside this book. If these thoughts are compelling, and you think that you might act on them, please tell someone close to you who can support you. You can also contact (in the UK – if you are elsewhere, please seek out equivalent resources in your country):

- your GP – they will work with you to put a plan in place to keep you safe
- the NHS out-of-hours service on 111 – they will help you to find the support that you need
- the Samaritans on 116 123 – they are available 24 hours a day, seven days a week, 365 days a year to speak to anyone who is thinking of suicide.

Please do not despair. We believe that you and your life are worthwhile, and we know that things can get better for you. Please keep on reading and seek whatever other support is appropriate.

A final word from the authors

We hope that this book will be of some help, whether on its own, or by inspiring you to seek face-to-face therapy, or as a companion to therapy, or as a refresher if you have already had therapy. However you use it, we hope that it will assist you in breaking free from depression and moving towards the life you want for yourself. We wish you well on this journey.

Michael and Michael
April 2020

1 What is depression?

Depression is depressingly common. If we have not suffered from it ourselves, then we probably know someone who has. And the statistics are alarming: 264 million people worldwide are currently diagnosed with depression, making it one of the three leading causes of disability worldwide (James et al., 2018). Clearly, too many people are becoming depressed.

What is less clear is why this is happening. Researchers disagree over whether we are in the midst of an epidemic of depression, perhaps brought on by our modern way of life, or whether we are just diagnosing it more, giving a new name to suffering that has always been with us. We don't need to take sides in this debate:

if you are suffering, we want to help, regardless of what words we use to describe the problem, or what we think caused it. But understanding a problem can help us to resolve it, and so in this chapter we will talk about how depression works, before moving on to solutions in the rest of the book.

Two views of depression

As with everything to do with the human mind, there are various theories of depression, and various ways of talking about it. We will discuss two of them here: the *medical model*, which is used in traditional healthcare settings and is probably somewhat familiar to you; and a *process model*, which is the sort that the third-wave therapies use, and that we will use in this book.

1. The medical model

In the medical model, depression is seen as an illness, which can be diagnosed using a list of symptoms, some of which are mental (e.g. feeling low) and some of which are physical (e.g. feeling tired). If you have a certain number of symptoms then you can be diagnosed with depression, which will be classified as mild, moderate or severe.

This can be a helpful way of thinking about depression. It helps doctors to quickly describe people's problems and know what treatment to offer, and many people find it a relief to hear that their experience can not only be named, but is quite common and is an illness. But the medical model has a negative focus – the aim is to cure an 'illness', rather than to promote flourishing that goes beyond the relief of symptoms. And it can all too easily become a trap: if we think that we have an illness called 'depression', we might start to identify with that label, and lose interest in understanding exactly what 'depression' consists of and what we can do about it. We might decide that it is a medical condition that we just have to live with, rather than something that we can address.

For these reasons, we do not make much use of the medical model here. We will use the word 'depression', but we use it loosely. We are less concerned with whether you tick the right boxes for a diagnosis of depression, and more interested in helping you to understand and work with your own particular experience.

2. A process model

Instead of carving up mental distress into distinct 'illnesses' such as depression, models of this sort focus on psychological *processes* that underlie these 'illnesses' and cut across them. On this view, the same processes can express themselves in a range of different ways, to produce a range of different 'mental illnesses'. So, depending on a person's character and circumstances, the same processes could show up as, for example, either depression, or anxiety, or post-traumatic stress disorder. An analogy might be heart disease, obesity and diabetes: three distinct illnesses that can all be caused by the same underlying process – too many calories that don't get burnt off.

The advantage of process models is that they focus directly on the psychological factors that drive depression, which makes them a good basis for psychological change. We can look beyond the label of 'depression', and see it not as an illness that you are stuck with until someone cures it for you, but rather as something that is created in each moment by what you do with your mind and body, and that you can start to work on right away. And, as you will see, our process-based approach goes beyond the negative focus of the medical model. Rather than stopping at the relief of symptoms, we will give you the tools to live even better than you did before depression arrived on the scene.

How depression works

We will focus on four psychological processes that can drive depression. They are not unique to depression or other forms of mental distress; rather, they are common to us all, because they arise from the way that the human mind has evolved over millions of years in order to help us to survive and thrive. But for some of us these processes can start to cause particular trouble, leading to depression and other types of distress, possibly because of how they play out in our fast-paced modern world.

1. Losing touch with the here-and-now

As we will explore in Chapter 2, most of us spend much of our time a million miles away, lost in memories, plans, daydreams, and conversations with ourselves. And this process tends to intensify in depression: we might get lost in endless spirals of thought about ourselves, our depression, where it all went so wrong, and what we need to do about it. We might spend very little of our time attending to what is happening right here, right now.

One problem with this is that if we don't notice what is actually happening in the present moment, then we can't make a conscious, wise choice about how to respond to it, and instead we act out of habit. And if we are suffering from depression, our habits are probably not helping us. Without awareness of the here-and-now, we will continue to act out the habits that trap us in depression.

And when we are not in the present moment, we are, by definition, lost in thought (our relationship to our thoughts is discussed in Chapter 3). In depression, our thinking is likely to be powerfully negative and self-critical – an effort to root out our flaws and fix them. But our efforts to think our way out of depression often pull us in deeper, into a process known as *rumination* – endlessly chewing over the same issues, seeking a resolution that never comes. And in this process we can construct and dwell endlessly upon a gloomy, restrictive narrative about ourselves (see Chapter 4). We allow it to define us, forgetting that we are much more than this story, and lose touch with the reality of the present moment, where we are free to act as we choose.

2. Struggling with thoughts and feelings

Much of the rumination that goes on in depression is in fact an effort to get rid of painful thoughts and feelings (see Chapters 3 and 5). We might argue with our thoughts, we might analyse our thoughts and feelings in the hope of gaining control over them, we might try to think our way to more pleasant thoughts and feelings, and we might decide to avoid situations that make us uncomfortable. Unfortunately, none of these strategies work for very long, if at all. Instead we get pulled further into our own thoughts, our emotions stubbornly resist our efforts at control, and in avoiding situations that trigger our painful thoughts and feelings, we end up avoiding the very things that we care about most.

A large part of the problem here is the relationship *between* thoughts and feelings. Our thoughts can trigger strong negative emotions even when nothing bad is actually happening, and then we take evasive action that only compounds depression. So when you approach something that matters to you – a social event, say, or applying for a job – your mind might fill up with predictions of disaster, which trigger painful feelings. You might get lost in thought, wrestling with your painful thoughts and feelings, trying to make them go away, and you might decide to simply back away from the whole situation, in order to gain some relief. In depression, this can become a pervasive and corrosive pattern of rumination and avoidance, that eats away at the meaning and joy in your life.

3. Being harsh and self-critical

Depression is often characterised by a profoundly harsh, critical and unfriendly attitude towards ourselves. As we will explain in Chapter 6, this makes it very hard to take the actions that would help us. When we attack ourselves and try to motivate ourselves with harsh, critical self-talk, we push ourselves into a defensive, threat-focused posture in which we are not inclined to try new things or take risks. Whereas when we are gentle and encouraging with ourselves, we create a sense of safety and willingness to explore. If you want to do the things that can free you from depression, it will be much easier with a kindly, compassionate attitude.

4. Not doing what matters

Freedom from depression is to be found in meaningful action, not in endless struggles to get your thoughts and feelings in order – this is the subject of Chapter 7. When we do what matters to us, regardless of what feelings show up, our lives are full and purposeful. Whereas when we try to seek out good feelings and get rid of bad ones, we get caught in efforts at emotional control that are doomed to fail and pull us away from the life that we want.

If you are suffering from depression, though, you may find that you don't even know what matters to you. You may have become so focused on avoiding your painful feelings and trying to think your way out of them that you rarely get anywhere near an activity that would enrich your life. And even when you do, you may be too preoccupied to notice. In depression, life can become a narrow, joyless retreat from pain, with no time, energy or motivation left to notice and move towards the things that you truly want. In Chapter 7, we will look at how you can identify and move towards those things.

How it works in practice

Let's look at an example of how these four processes play out.

Anthony is planning to go out to a party, for the first time in a while. He has been feeling low and avoiding people since his girlfriend broke up with him. As he starts to get ready, he thinks, 'You'll probably be in a bad mood when you're there. You'll drag the evening down.' He feels a sinking feeling as he imagines others talking to him but secretly wishing he was not there. He tries to prove himself wrong by thinking of times when he went out feeling low but then had a good time anyway. He comes up with one such memory, but also remembers his ex-girlfriend saying that he wasn't much fun. 'People find me boring', he thinks, and sits down with his head in his hands, because he suspects that he is, at heart, a very boring person. He doesn't want to see his friends at all now, and thinks that he'll lie down in bed, just for a minute, until he feels better. He doesn't feel better though – his mind keeps going over the question of whether or not he is boring, and every time he thinks of going to the party he feels a fresh stab of fear and shame. He stays in bed, ignores messages from his friends asking where he is, and looks at the internet on his phone, trying to distract himself from thoughts about how boring he is and how pathetic he is for not going to the party.

Anthony, in this example, is confronted by an opportunity to do something that matters to him: to socialise and connect with others. His thoughts, however, have other ideas, and predict disaster, which triggers painful feelings (*losing touch with the here-*

and-now). Anthony tries to get rid of these thoughts and feelings with further thinking, but it doesn't work, and in fact makes his pain more intense (*losing touch with the here-and-now; struggling with thoughts and feelings*). So he retreats from it by getting into bed (*not doing what matters*), where he gets lost in self-criticism (*being harsh and self-critical*) and efforts to distract himself with the internet (*struggling with thoughts and feelings*), thus avoiding the very thing that he truly wants – connection with others (*not doing what matters*). This is the pattern that has pulled Anthony into depression since his breakup with his girlfriend.

This way of thinking about depression might seem strange or confusing, in which case please don't worry – we are not expecting you to grasp or remember it right away. Everything will become much clearer as we move through the book, looking in more detail at the processes that drive depression and the skills that you need to work with them. And if you feel lost at any point, please remember to be kind to yourself.

Trying to be happy

As you might notice in the example above, it is an unfortunate irony that much of our suffering arises precisely from our attempts to be happy. Anthony just wants to feel better, and so he thinks hard about his problems, tries to talk himself out of his negative thinking, stays away from situations that frighten him, and distracts himself with the immediate gratification of the internet. Even his self-criticism, in a perverse way, is part of an effort to be happy, or at least to avoid more pain: he might be trying to motivate himself to do better; or reminding himself of (what he thinks is) his place in the world, so that he doesn't get above himself and get cut down to size.

This is probably true for you, too; your efforts to feel better are probably making things worse. And so in this book we are going to ask you to try something different. But before we lay out our approach, it will be helpful to complete Exercise 1.1 on the next page, which asks you to have a look at what you have tried so far, and whether or not it has been working. If it has, then great, keep going. But if not, then this book is for you.

As will always be the case, we present this exercise with no wish to make you feel bad, or to blame you for your difficulties. The processes that drive depression are common to everyone, and so we know first-hand how hard it can be to do what matters when our thoughts and feelings get in the way. But we also know that seeing clearly the effects of what we have been doing is the first step towards changing it.

Have a go at answering the questions below, and then filling in a table as in the example given – you can make one yourself. We have included an example from Anthony, who we just met. You will notice Anthony's strategies for getting rid of painful thoughts and feelings listed in the central column ('What do I do to get rid of these thoughts and feelings?').

Exercise 1.1

How do you deal with painful thoughts and feelings?

- What thoughts and feelings (meaning both emotions and body sensations) do you find most difficult in your life? Perhaps there are one or two that you would most like to get rid of. For example, thoughts such as, 'I'm not good enough,' or, 'I'm unlovable', and feelings such as lethargy, sadness or shame.

- What have you done to avoid or get rid of these thoughts and feelings? This might include big things, such as moving jobs or countries; small things, such as comfort eating or surfing the internet; and internal things, such as trying to think your way out of your thoughts and feelings.

- What have been the consequences of these actions in the short and the long term? Have they worked? Have your feelings gone away for good, or do they keep coming back? Have these actions cost you anything in terms of your quality of life?

Thoughts and feelings that I want to get rid of	What I do to get rid of these thoughts and feelings	What are the consequences in the short & long term?	
		Short term	Long term
Thoughts I'm boring.' I'll drag the evening down.' I'll feel more tired at the party.' **Emotions** Sadness, loneliness, shame. **Body sensations** Tiredness.	Don't go to the party; stay at home in bed. Don't respond to messages from my friends. Problem-solve, worry and beat myself up. Distract myself with my phone.	I felt relieved and less worried. I felt like I was really focusing on fixing my problems, which felt good. I enjoyed surfing the internet, and it took my mind off my problem and how bad I felt.	I feel more upset, sad, guilty and lonely now as I didn't see my friends. Avoiding all my friends lately has affected my friendships – people have stopped contacting me so much. I felt more tired but also unable to sleep after thinking hard and surfing the internet. I am falling behind with things because I waste a lot of time dwelling on my problems and surfing the internet.

In doing this exercise, you may notice that some of your own attempts to deal with painful thoughts and feelings do not get rid of them for good, and can become traps. They pull you away from the here-and-now, into rumination, self-criticism and struggles with your thoughts and feelings. They leave you with little time and energy for the things that you truly want to do, and keep you from being the person that you want to be. While they may provide short-term relief, in the longer term they undermine your quality of life.

If that is true for you, again please don't be hard on yourself. That will just make you feel worse and want to avoid the whole situation, for example by not finishing this book! We all struggle with these processes, and many of us will experience depression at some point in our lives. And it is not our fault: we did not design the human mind, or the complicated world in which we find ourselves, and we did not choose the circumstances that we, as individuals, were born into. But it *is* our responsibility, because no one except us can take charge of our minds, our habits and our complicated lives, and take them in the directions that matter most to us.

So how, exactly, do we do that?

A recipe for change

In order to break free from depression, we will show you how to:

F – ocus on what is right here, right now

R – elease your struggle with thoughts and feelings

E – ncourage yourself with a kindly attitude

E – ngage in action according to what matters to you.

All of which, helpfully, spells **FREE**. Keep this in mind as a way to remember the skills that you will learn in this book.

In more detail, this will mean learning how to:

- wake up to the present moment and regain intentional control over your life, rather than blindly following the dictates of habit (Chapter 2)
- step back from your thoughts instead of struggling with them and being controlled by them (Chapter 3)
- recognise that you are more than the story that you tell about yourself, and that it need not limit you (Chapter 4)
- turn towards your feelings with an attitude of kindness and curiosity, instead of habitually trying to get away from them (Chapter 5)

- treat yourself kindly (Chapter 6)
- work out what truly matters to you – what you can do to bring meaning and joy to your life (Chapter 7)
- do what matters to you (Chapter 7).

As we have said above, don't worry if some of this is confusing or sounds strange – all will be explained. And remember, the only way to know if it will work for you is to try it and see.

Ready? Then let's begin.

2 Turning the lights on

To address any problem, including depression, you need awareness of it. You need to see clearly what happens, why it happens and what the consequences are. And to do that, you need to focus your attention upon the problem.

In the last chapter, we focused on depression and started to build up awareness of how it works by *thinking* about it – we introduced you to some ideas about depression and asked you to think about how they apply to your own life. But we also told you that thinking can be part of the problem in depression, and in many other forms of mental distress – that you can easily become trapped in endless rumination on why it is happening, what it means and what you can do about it. So what, you may wonder, are you supposed to do? How are you supposed to understand depression without thinking about it?

The answer is not that you should try to stop thinking, but rather that, in order to avoid getting lost in your thinking, it should be balanced by another form of awareness – *present-moment awareness*. Which in turn is supported by *flexible attention* – the ability to pay attention to what you want, when you want.

Present-moment awareness and flexible attention

Present-moment awareness is always available to us. It is simply noticing (rather than thinking about) what is happening right here, right now, using your five senses. It is like turning on the lights and seeing what is in front of you. Let's try it.

Exercise 2.1
Noticing the present moment

- ■ Take a moment to become aware of what is happening right here, right now.

- ■ Notice where you are sitting.

- ■ Notice what you can see. Notice the sounds you can hear. Notice what you can smell. Notice the sensations of your feet touching the floor, the sensations of your clothes touching your skin, and the sensations of this book touching your hands.

It's that simple! While you were doing the exercise, you were aware of what is right here, right now. And in order to notice different aspects of the present moment, you used flexible attention: you deliberately moved your attention from sights, to sounds, to smells, to sensations. If awareness is like a floodlight that illuminates the present moment, then attention is like a torch beam that picks out particular elements of it.

Present-moment awareness versus thinking

As simple as it is, we usually spend little of our time paying attention in this way. Instead, our attention hops from thing to thing, often without us even noticing, let alone consciously directing it. And in particular it is captured by our thoughts, which pull us away from the present moment – we go about in a kind of dream of thought, endlessly remembering, planning, and talking to ourselves (or other people) in our heads. You probably know what it is like to be physically here, but mentally somewhere else.

Even when we do focus on the here-and-now, we tend to focus on our *thoughts* about it. We tell ourselves an endless story about whatever is happening – a sort of running commentary in our heads – explaining it, comparing it to other things, deciding how much we like it and how we might like it to be instead. And in consequence we might fail to notice exactly what is going on right here, right now.

Let's have a closer look at the difference between *thinking* and just *noticing* what is right here, right now:

Exercise 2.2
Thinking versus noticing

- Think about breathing. You might think about how breathing works: the role of the lungs, the diaphragm, and so on. You might think about how breathing keeps you alive. You might think about how many breaths you take in a day. You might even evaluate breathing. Is it useful? Is it pleasant?

- Now just *feel* your breathing as it is, in this moment. See if you can tune in to the physical sensations of breathing. Notice the sensations of air entering your nostrils as you breathe in. Your stomach deflating as you breathe out. Now, see if you can pay this level of attention to 20 breaths in a row.

In doing this exercise, you might have noticed the difference between thinking about the breath and experiencing it directly, by feeling its sensations.

You might also have noticed how hard it is to stay in the present moment for long. Your thoughts keep coming, and before too long they capture your attention and pull you into a train of thought. The lights of awareness go out. After a while, they flick on again – you remember what you were supposed to be doing and redirect your attention to the breath. It stays there for a few more moments, before thoughts pull you away once again.

This is nothing to feel bad about – everyone's mind is like that! But perhaps you can see how strong the habit of unawareness is, and how hard it is to pay attention on purpose. If we want to spend more time in the present moment, attending to what we choose to, then we need to cultivate the habits of waking up to the present moment, and develop some control over our attention. And if we can do that, then we can begin to work on *all* of our habits, including the ones that maintain depression. Let's explore how this works.

Autopilot

When we are lost in thought, we are not aware of what is happening right here, right now, and so we cannot make conscious choices about how to respond to it. Nor can we notice the consequences of our actions and decide to do something different next time. Instead we act automatically, out of habit. We can call this state *autopilot*.

For example, most of us have had the experience of driving, or walking, or cycling, and arriving at our destination with almost no memory of the journey, because for most of it our attention was elsewhere – on our memories, plans and daydreams. How do we manage the complex task of driving without paying any attention to it? By relying on *habits* that we have built up through many hours of driving. This is a fabulous ability – we can do a remarkable range of things remarkably well without paying any conscious attention to them, using our well-trained habits. This frees up our attention for other things and stops us having to figure everything out afresh each time we do it.

But we can run into trouble when we rely on autopilot too much, because our habits may not always serve us well. Perhaps you have some bad habits as a driver, and as a result you have several points on your licence; and suppose you wanted to improve your driving, perhaps because of those points. You might have a good think about the problem: what kind of driver you are, and how you got to be that way; other drivers on the road; the Highway Code. Eventually, you might come up with an understanding of where you are going wrong, and a plan for fixing it.

So far, so good. But if, the next time you get into your car, you go straight into autopilot and are barely aware of what you are doing throughout the journey, how are you going to implement your plan? You won't be able to; instead you will be relying on your automatic, unconscious habits to get you to your destination. And so you will probably drive just as you always have. Or you could even wind up being distracted from your driving in the present moment by thoughts about your driving and your plan to improve it!

And it gets worse: maybe your analysis of your driving and your plan to improve it are not that great after all. You have done your best to analyse your driving, but if you never pay any attention to your driving while you are actually doing it, how would you know what you are doing wrong, and why? You might not even be aware of most of the unsafe, inconsiderate things that you do, let alone have noticed the circumstances in which you tend to do them, or how other drivers react to them.

The power of the present moment

Suppose that, instead of losing yourself in your analysis, you set about paying attention while you drive.

You might notice all sorts of things: that you tend to drive too fast when you are in a rush or a bad mood, that when you see an amber light you feel a surge of adrenaline and your shoulders tense before you accelerate through it, and that you then get stuck in the middle of an intersection and end up blocking other drivers.

Having noticed all of this using the power of present-moment awareness, you could use that same power to change your behaviour. When you see the amber light, you might notice the surge of adrenaline and the tensing of your muscles and make a conscious choice to relax and stop at the lights. Or if you do rush through the lights and get stuck in the intersection, you might notice the drivers you have inconvenienced and give them a wave of apology, and someone might wave back to signal that it's okay.

Let's see how your habits are showing up right now, as you read this book.

Exercise 2.3
Noticing habits

- Take a moment to notice where you are right now.

- Notice how you are sitting; you probably sit in this position habitually.

- Notice where you are sitting; you probably didn't give your choice of seat much thought – you probably chose it out of habit.

- Now change your position or your seat, if you can, to one that is not habitual for you.

- Notice what that feels like.

In doing this exercise, you have stepped out of autopilot and into present-moment awareness. You have consciously brought your attention to where and how you are sitting, rather than just doing it habitually. And you have, perhaps, realised that you have many other options when it comes to sitting, which you do not usually notice and explore. And then you made a conscious choice to do something different. If this is true of something as simple as sitting, what might it mean about other areas of your life?

Depression and the present moment

In the last chapter, we listed four psychological processes that underlie depression: losing touch with the present moment, struggling with thoughts and feelings, treating yourself harshly, and not doing what matters. You might be surprised to hear that they are all habits – things that you have done many times and that have now become automatic, so that they repeat themselves endlessly without you intending to do them, noticing yourself doing them, or noticing their consequences.

These are habits that we all have, but if you are suffering from depression, they are likely to have taken on an especially powerful and pernicious role in your life. You might spend a lot of your time lost in ruminative thought, trying to think your way out of your painful thoughts and feelings. You might seek refuge from your thoughts and feelings in unhelpful distractions such as overeating, the internet, drink or drugs. You might find yourself pulling back from situations that you care about, such as relationships with others or work opportunities, because they seem to carry too much risk of failure, rejection and pain. You might be very hard on yourself. And you might not see these habits as a problem, because you do not notice how they are affecting you and your life. And even if you do notice, it might feel like you have no other option, because all of this *just happens*, without you noticing it as it happens.

With present-moment awareness and flexible attention, you can notice yourself acting out these unhelpful habits (or feeling the urge to). You can notice their triggers and their effects, just as you did in Exercise 1.1 (*see p22*). You can notice what really matters to you in the situation in which you find yourself, and then you can make a conscious choice to move towards it, instead of automatically acting out the habits of depression. Over time, you can build up new, more helpful habits: of awareness, of allowing your thoughts and feelings to come and go without struggle, of taking the actions that you truly want to, and of treating yourself with kindness.

Let's see how all of this works in practice.

Judy has felt low for much of her life, but lately it has been getting worse. She is at home, trying to cook a meal for her young son, who is overtired and needs to go to bed. This would not be happening if her husband was here, but he is away on a work trip. Judy has tried to suggest that he travels less so that he can help at home more and allow her to work more, but he tends to get upset and angry, saying that she is accusing him of being a bad father, which makes Judy back off. She has always found it hard to say things that upset others; it makes her feel guilty, and so she tends to avoid conflict and tries to be helpful, so that others will be happy and her relationships with them harmonious. She is thinking hard about the situation. She thinks about her relationship with her husband, and further back to her childhood – she suspects that she finds it hard to stand up to people because her father was so domineering. She thinks about how long she has been feeling down, and how unable she is to change it, and how pathetic that makes her. Her phone rings and it's her husband. He asks how she is doing, and she says fine, and gets off the phone quickly. When she finally manages to give her son his dinner, he cries because it is too hot – she did not think to check the temperature because she was caught up in thoughts about her husband. She has the thought that she is a bad mother, which upsets her, and she starts thinking of other ways that she has let her son down, while he eats his meal and tries to get her attention.

With present-moment awareness and flexible control over her attention, things might have gone differently for Judy. When her husband arranged his trip abroad, she might have noticed her autopilot urge to agree to it and chosen instead to challenge him. She might have done the same when he phoned while she was cooking her son's dinner, either telling him it wasn't a good time, or perhaps not even answering. And she might have noticed herself disappearing into harsh, self-critical rumination while her son was seeking her attention, and been able instead to focus on the present moment and engage with him.

Cultivating present-moment awareness and flexible attention

Present-moment awareness needs to become a new habit – we need to connect with it so often that it starts to happen by itself. And flexible control over attention is like a muscle that gets stronger with repeated use. So you will need to practise. Neither present-moment awareness nor flexible attention will magically grow stronger just from reading about them and understanding what they are.

But before we go any further, a word of reassurance. If you are worried about letting go of your existing habits – don't be. You will develop new habits, but your old ones will still be available to you if you need them (and they may well be helpful in some situations). The human brain does not have a 'delete' button, so in building new habits you are expanding your repertoire, rather than getting rid of its existing contents.

With that said, let's begin. We recommend that you try both of the following brief exercises, and then practise them several times each day – they need not take more than a minute or two.

Exercise 2.4

Connect with the present moment, whatever you are doing

With this exercise you can build the habit of present-moment awareness, and also practise moving your attention about at will.

You can come into awareness at any time, during any activity, and explore your present-moment experience. You can do it right now, with this book.

- First of all, notice how you are sitting.

- Now notice the book (or device) in your hands.

- Feel the weight of it in your hands. Feel the texture of it.

- Now look at it closely. Really take in the shape of it, the light and shade on its surface, the colours.

- Now see if it smells of anything.

- Hold it up to your ear and see if it makes a sound (you may have to rub its surface or bend the pages to get a sound out of it), or just acknowledge the silence coming from the book.

- Notice how your body feels.

Do this often, with other objects, or whatever you can see, hear, smell, taste and feel. You don't need to stop whatever you are doing, just start to notice your present-moment sensory experience of it.

Exercise 2.5

Anchor yourself in the present moment

With this exercise you practise connecting with the present moment and maintaining steady attention.

- Pick something to focus on, here and now. It could be the sensations of your feet as you walk, or the sound of the traffic outside.

- Hold your attention there, as best you can. Whenever your mind wanders, just bring it back to your chosen focus.

- Don't try too hard. Your mind will wander again and again; just keep bringing it gently back again and again.

- It is fine to notice other things as well – it isn't possible to block them out – but try to keep your chosen object of attention somewhere in your awareness.

Finally, try at least one of the following longer exercises, and consider making it a new habit to do one of them each day, for at least 10 minutes.

Exercise 2.6
Mindful breathing

This is probably the oldest way to train your awareness and attention. It is a meditation that people have been doing for at least 2,000 years!

- Sit comfortably, or lie down.

- Close your eyes or, if you prefer to leave them open, lower your gaze.

■ Tune into the physical sensations of breathing, either at the abdomen or at the chest.

■ Keep paying attention to the sensations of breathing, as best you can. When your mind wanders, which it certainly will, just gently bring it back to the breath.

■ Don't try too hard – that won't help. Each time the mind wanders, just gently return to the breath, using it as an anchor to the present moment. And when the mind wanders, there is no need to give yourself a hard time – you are just a normal person, with a normal, wandering mind.

Exercise 2.7
Mindful walking

This is an exercise that you do while walking, which means that you can use it out and about as well as during your dedicated practice time. It can be a good exercise to use if staying still feels too difficult at the moment.

■ Find a space in which you can walk back and forth. Or, if you are out and about, just apply the instructions below while walking as normal.

- Take a step, perhaps a bit more slowly than you usually would, and try to tune into the physical sensations of walking. You could feel the soles of your feet coming up off the ground and making contact with it. Or you could feel the whole of the foot. Or your ankles, knees, hips or any other body part. The idea is simply to walk while paying attention to the physical sensations of walking.

- When you notice that your mind has wandered, which it certainly will, just bring your attention back to the physical sensations of walking. And don't get self-critical when your mind wanders – everyone's mind wanders. And if you do notice yourself getting self-critical, don't criticise yourself for that!

Planning to practise

To develop present-moment awareness and flexible attention, you will need to practise, and you are more likely to practise if you have a plan.

Think about how you are going to train your awareness and attention every day.

- Which shorter exercises will you do? What events in your day could remind you to do them? For example, you might do them when you arrive at work and when you get home, or as you are waiting for the kettle to boil, or at red lights. Could you set reminders on your phone?

■ Will you set time aside each day for a longer exercise? If so, what time of day will you do it? Are there any special arrangements that you need to make, such as asking others not to disturb you?

■ You might find it helpful to use an app to help you practise the skills in this chapter. There are some excellent mindfulness apps available that can guide you through various ways of training your present-moment awareness and flexible attention. See our *Further resources* section for some suggestions.

Turning the lights on

Depression is a dark place to be. Your thoughts and feelings are gloomy, and the world looks thoroughly bleak. But also you are *in the dark*. You are acting out unhelpful habits without awareness of what you are doing and how it affects your life. And if you do momentarily snap out of autopilot and notice what is happening, quickly the spotlight of your attention is pulled away by your negative thoughts, and you disappear again into the darkness of unawareness. In this chapter, we have offered techniques for beginning to turn on the lights of awareness and take control of the torch beam of attention. If you can build these new skills, then you will be in a position to see your life more clearly and make wise choices, rather than bumping about in the dark.

Summary

- Remember that awareness of things in the present moment is different from thinking about them.

- By checking in with the present moment, you can start to notice and change your habits.

- In particular, take care to notice the habits of depression: lack of awareness, struggling with thoughts and feelings, treating yourself harshly and not doing what matters.

- Developing flexible attention will help you to maintain your present-moment awareness and focus on the things that matter to you.

3 Surfing your mind

You might be getting the idea that our thoughts are the villain of this story: they pull us away from the present moment and mire us in rumination, rendering us unable to see what is actually going on and to respond appropriately. And it gets worse, as we shall see: they mislead us, torment us, waste our time and energy, and tell us to do unwise things. Our thoughts, it might seem, are the source of our difficulties.

But a major insight of the third-wave therapies is that there is nothing wrong with our thoughts. Thoughts themselves cannot cause us any problems. It is our *relationship* with them that can. Specifically, our tendency to buy into them, get stuck to them, struggle with them, and let them control what we do. If we could hold our thoughts more lightly, seeing them as mere products of our mind, some of which are helpful and some of which are not, rather than as indisputable truths or commandments, we could avoid all of this trouble. In this chapter, we will explore the difficulties that we get into with our thoughts, and how we can build a healthier relationship with them, in which we are able to:

- step back from our thoughts
- stop struggling with our thoughts
- choose how much to engage with our thoughts
- do what we truly want to, instead of what our thoughts tell us to.

Surfing the internet – and your mind

The internet is a fantastic tool – an incredible, bottomless treasure trove of information and ideas, without which we would find it impossible to function in the modern world. But it is a bit too compelling. We are addicted to it – to the clickbait articles, the insecurity-inducing social media posts, the fake news, the endless arguments. All too often, the internet wastes our time, winds us up, fills our heads with bad ideas and fake news, and pulls us away from doing the things that really matter to us. We talk about surfing the internet, but sadly the way we use it is not much like surfing.

Surfers pick just the right wave, catch it at just the right moment, and ride it with great skill. Whereas the internet sucks us in like a riptide – we just cannot resist it, and the more we click, the better the algorithms get at serving up more content that keeps us hooked.

Your thinking mind, too, is a fantastic problem-solving tool, fashioned over many millions of years by evolution. With it, we can do what no other animal can, and it has made us the most successful species on the planet. We can remember the past, imagine and plan for the future, develop complex abstract theories, think in detail about ourselves and others, and even have imagined conversations with those others. And we do all of this in sophisticated verbal language. Take a moment to look around you, wherever you are, and imagine how different things would be if humans had never evolved our distinctive ability to solve problems with our minds. How much of what you see around you could have been created without this amazing ability?

But we often relate to our minds in an unhelpful way, just as we do the internet. Too often our attention is caught by a compelling thought, and minutes or hours later we wake up to the present moment, to find that we've been lost in thought, moving from idea to memory to worry to imaginary argument with someone, clicking and clicking on the mind's links, in an out-of-control binge.

And in depression, we binge upon the most disturbing content: bad memories, imagined future disasters, negative comparisons of ourselves to others, and arguments with ourselves that go nowhere. And the more we click, the more the mind's algorithm serves up more of the same: 'If you liked *You're a failure*, you might also like *Nobody wants you*'; 'Because you watched *Memory of embarrassing yourself at school,* check out the *Shameful memories* channel'. We lose ourselves in whirlpools of thought that make us miserable, distort our perceptions of the world, waste our time, and take us away from doing things that we care about. In short, we ruminate, and avoid the real world and our real lives.

Take a look at the following example.

> Rupert is lying in bed. He tells himself that he should get up, but then tells himself that he knows he won't, so he should just give up on the idea. He presses the pillow over his face. He thinks that he has been feeling like this for so long that he should just give up on any hope of it changing. He thinks back to how he used to be, once upon a time, and how happy he was. How overconfident. He now thinks that was just a brief interlude, and starts thinking about when he was younger, at school, which sets off a series of painful memories of rejection and humiliation. These thoughts are just going to drag him down, he thinks. All this self-indulgent, self-pitying thinking.

He deserves to be depressed. He is contemptible. He thinks about getting up, but once all these thoughts have started up, they won't stop, so there's no point. Even if he does go to work, he'll be in a terrible state and unable to talk to anyone in a normal way, he thinks. They already think he is odd, and easy to push around. Just like at school. Better to stay home and not let everyone know how bad things are. Another painful memory comes into his mind. They aren't going to stop now, he thinks, and he rolls over, grunting into his pillow with frustration and misery. 'Go away!' he thinks, addressing his thoughts. 'GO AWAY!' The thoughts don't go away.

Let's have a look at some of the ways that Rupert (like all of us) gets into trouble with his thoughts.

Tools, not truths

We tend to believe in our thoughts. Of course we do! When we say, 'I think X', we mean, 'I believe X to be true'. But can it really be the case that every thought that passes through your mind is a faithful guide to reality? If you have ever changed your mind about anything, you must have had one set of thoughts that you believed in, and then rejected them in favour of another set. Both sets of thoughts can't have been true. And consider the people around you: do you believe all of *their* thoughts to be true? Do you believe that Rupert's mind is telling him the total, unvarnished truth about everything? Probably not. But then what about your own mind? Is it likely that you are the only human being ever to have lived whose mind serves up truthful thoughts 100% of the time?

Instead, we suggest that your thoughts are rather like the endless opinions that proliferate on the internet: you can find just about anything on there, and while there is some gold, there is also a lot of dross. But it can be tempting to believe everything you read, especially when it agrees with everything else that appears in your echo chamber. On the other hand, trying to separate out your true thoughts from your false thoughts would be as endless a task as it would on the internet – for every argument, there is a counterargument, and it is impossible to know who to believe. And so we return to the idea of *workability*. Instead of trying to discover *the truth*, simply ask yourself whether any given thought is workable: ask whether continuing to engage with it moves you in a direction that you want to go.

This gives us an important perspective on thoughts. They are just products of your mind, which may or may not be helpful. They are tools, not truths. Treat your thoughts as what they are and you can put them to work for you, instead of the other way around.

Exercise 3.1
Your changing mind

■ Think of three thoughts that you have had in the past that you no longer believe to be true. Perhaps when you were younger you believed that Santa Claus was real. Perhaps you thought something would go wrong, but then it was okay. Or perhaps you thought something would be okay, but then it went wrong. Perhaps sometimes you have positive thoughts, and sometimes you have negative thoughts on the same topic. For example, sometimes you might think, 'I'm great at my job', and at other times you might think, 'I'm hopeless at my job'.

■ If you have ever had thoughts that have changed, what does all this say about your thoughts? Can they always be true? Could you ever know for sure which are true and which are not?

Old brain, new brain

It is possible to very roughly divide the brain up into the parts that do the thinking, which evolved relatively recently, and the parts that handle our feelings and body responses, which are much older. The problem is that these different parts of the brain don't always work together smoothly, because evolution has not yet had time to iron out the glitches, let alone adapt to the modern world.

Because of this, our thoughts can *feel* all too real: quite often we react to them, physically and emotionally, as though they were real threats. You will know this if you have ever thought of something frightening and felt your heart rate accelerate, adrenaline flood your body, and your stomach turn over. That is the 'fight or flight' response – your body is quite literally preparing to run from or fight off a physical threat. But there's nothing to run from or fight! Except your own thoughts. But the more ancient parts of our brains don't know that, and treat alarming thoughts as though they were real, live threats.

This is a large part of why struggling with our feelings is such a problem for us. Unlike other animals, the feelings that make us want to move away from something (keeping us safe from real-life threats) can be triggered by nothing more than our own thoughts, and then we take action to make those feelings go away – action that often doesn't take us where we really want to go in life. How do you imagine Rupert is feeling as he lies in bed, imagining going to work and what his colleagues will think of him? He feels the pain of a humiliation that has not actually happened, except in his mind, but it is enough to make him avoid his workplace and his colleagues. And while the situation that triggered Rupert's painful feelings was only imaginary, the costs of avoiding his workplace are real: his professional prospects will be harmed if he misses work too often, his relationships with his colleagues will be harmed if he avoids them, and he loses the opportunity to learn that in fact his painful thoughts and feelings are not real threats – they are just thoughts and feelings.

Exercise 3.2

Triggered!

■ What are two or three ideas you have about yourself that are strongly tied to your depression? (E.g. 'I'm unlovable', 'I'm not good enough', 'I am no good at my job'.)

■ Let them come into your mind, and think about them for a few moments.

■ Notice what happens to your emotional state. Notice what happens in your body.

■ Now notice what urge arises; what do you feel like doing next? (E.g. avoiding people, working longer and harder, eating unhealthy food.)

■ Would that be a move towards or away from the things that really matter to you in life?

Your mind has a mind of its own

If we treat everything that our thoughts tell us as both true and real, it is going to seem important to get our thoughts in order, as Rupert tries to. We will want to create a coherent account of ourselves and the world around us, which explains who we are and how we got to be that way, and we will want upsetting thoughts to go away. We might try to control and suppress certain thoughts, or to try to replace them with more positive thoughts, or start sorting through and debating them in an effort to decide what we *really* think – what is really the truth about ourselves and our lives.

These efforts are about as productive as arguments on the internet: they go on forever, consuming time, energy and attention, and no one is left any the wiser. In fact, they are positively unhelpful, because they take us away from the real business of living lives that are meaningful and satisfying. Would you rather argue on the internet about how people ought to live, and shout down everyone you disagree with, or would you rather shut your laptop and actually *live* in whatever way you think is best?

You cannot control your mind or beat it in debate, at least not for long. Such efforts just focus your attention on the very thought patterns or ideas that you are fighting against, which stimulates the mind to produce more content on those themes. Any thought that you try to suppress tends to come back more strongly, and any argument that you make against your mind will be met by a counterargument, if not now, then before too long. You might seem to enjoy a victory every now and again, but it is only temporary: your mind has at least as much stamina as you do, and you cannot get away from it.

Let's test this out by trying to control your mind.

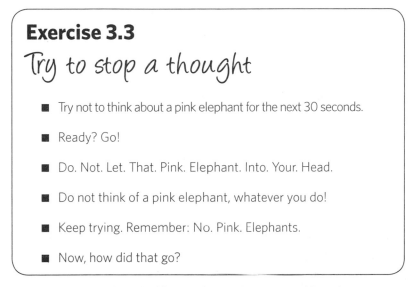

Exercise 3.3

Try to stop a thought

■ Try not to think about a pink elephant for the next 30 seconds.

■ Ready? Go!

■ Do. Not. Let. That. Pink. Elephant. Into. Your. Head.

■ Do not think of a pink elephant, whatever you do!

■ Keep trying. Remember: No. Pink. Elephants.

■ Now, how did that go?

What happened? Probably, you found that you could not keep the thought of a pink elephant out of your mind for very long. You discovered that you cannot control your mind with brute force.

You might be surprised, however, to learn that *we* can control your mind. That might sound unlikely, but, trust us, you'll see. We know exactly what you are going to think while doing the next exercise. Ready? Okay, here we go...

Exercise 3.4
We can control your mind

Read the following sentence:

Mary had a little ...

What word popped into your mind? Was it by any chance 'lamb'?

This is not just a gimmick or party trick. Rather, it reveals something very important about your mind: it is constantly linking one thing to another, and then it uses those links to produce thoughts, automatically, in response to whatever is going on around you or within you. So, if you have learned that 'Mary had a little' is linked to 'lamb', then when you hear the first part of the sentence, you cannot stop your mind from completing it. And this is what your mind does all day long: pretty much everything you see, hear, touch, taste, smell, feel or think will automatically set off a thought in your mind, which will set off another linked thought, and so on. For Rupert, thoughts of past happiness are linked to thoughts about past *un*happiness, and one painful memory is linked to another, and another. So, once this train of thought has been set in motion, it runs along this well-established track. Rupert has probably been over the same territory in his mind many times, and his efforts to think his way out of it are doomed to fail.

This could seem disheartening – it might seem that if you cannot control your mind, you are destined to be forever at its mercy. But in fact, nothing could be further from the truth. First, as we saw in Chapter 2, we can step off the train of thought by connecting with the here-and-now. Without the fuel of our attention, the train runs out of steam. And second, even if the train keeps on running, no matter, because, as we are about to see, just as you cannot control your mind, *it* need not control *you*.

Never mind your mind!

This is the punchline to the points we have laid out so far. Just as you don't have to believe in your thoughts, *neither do you have to do what they say*, any more than you have to follow whatever advice you might read on an internet forum. You can think one thing and do quite another, and thus live a life that is not constrained by whatever thoughts happen to come into your mind. Rupert could have had all the same thoughts in the example above, and yet got up and gone to work. Don't believe us? Try this:

Exercise 3.5
Your mind need not control you

- While holding this book, think to yourself, 'I cannot hold this book'.

- Think it as hard as you can. Repeat it over and over, and really mean it.

- But keep on holding the book.

See? It is entirely possible to think something, and yet do the exact opposite. But much of the time we forget this, and blindly treat our thoughts as both truths and commands. If our mind tells us that we will suffer humiliation if we go to work, we believe it, and then when it tells us to stay at home in bed, we do so. And little by little we give up the activities that give us meaning and satisfaction, because that is what our minds tell us we must do. It does not have to be this way: we can learn to recognise what it is that we really want in life (more on this in Chapter 7) and treat our thoughts as potential tools to help us move in that direction, rather than seeing them as the last word on what we can or should do.

Getting unstuck

It is, of course, not so simple as us just *telling* you that you don't have to obey your thoughts. Even if we understand that thoughts need not control us, applying that understanding takes some work. This is because the habit of being glued to our thoughts is powerful, and because we often don't even notice it happening. In fact, much of the time we don't even notice that we are *thinking*. We are so used to looking at the world through our thoughts that we forget they are there, like a lens over the torch beam of our attention, distorting and colouring our perceptions, and controlling what we do.

To move towards the kind of life we want, we need to get unstuck from our thoughts. We need to:

- notice *that* we are thinking, and *what* we are thinking
- see our thoughts *as thoughts* (rather than facts or commands that we must obey)
- choose whether or not to follow their suggestions, according to whether it takes us in a direction we want to go.

If we can do all this, then we can be like a surfer in the ocean: watching the waves, picking the right ones to ride, and knowing when to jump off.

You have already begun this process with the exercises in the last chapter. As soon as you connect with the present moment, you have noticed that you are thinking, and stepped back from your thoughts. You can take a look at the situation you are in, and the thoughts that are being produced by your mind, and decide whether engaging with them is helping you to do what matters in that moment.

Here are some exercises to take this process further. Remember that you will need to practise them several times each day, including when things are going well, so that you will be ready to use them at more difficult times – you need a lot of practice before you surf the biggest waves.

But first, a word of caution: when our clients begin using these techniques, they are sometimes disappointed to find that painful thoughts do not disappear or stop being painful. But the aim of getting unstuck from thoughts is not to feel better, and certainly not to do the impossible and get rid of unwanted thoughts; it is to see things more clearly and *choose* your actions more freely, rather than being under the helpless control of your thoughts.

Exercise 3.6
Clouds in the sky

■ Close your eyes, or lower your gaze, and see if you can notice the thoughts passing through your mind, as though they were clouds passing across the sky.

■ If you don't seem to notice any, just wait – they will show up. You might think, 'There aren't any!' or, 'This doesn't work!' Notice that those are thoughts – just clouds passing across the sky.

■ As thoughts come into your mind, you will repeatedly find yourself carried away by them; rather than noticing your thoughts, you will just be *thinking* them. When you notice that happening, step back from your thoughts and start noticing them once again, just like clouds in the sky.

■ Do this for a few minutes, or as long as you like.

With this exercise, your thoughts become just another thing to notice, here and now, along with sights, sounds, smells and bodily sensations. You might find that when you see thoughts like this, as words and pictures passing through your awareness, you also see that you don't have to be controlled by them, any more than you would be controlled by a voice that you could hear on the radio, or a film projected onto a screen.

Exercise 3.7
Naming thought patterns

Are there any thoughts, or patterns of thought, that you find yourself getting repeatedly stuck to? Ones that seem to recur often, take control of you, and interfere with your life? If so, try giving them names. The names can be whatever you like, from the descriptive – e.g. 'worrying', 'self-criticism' or 'work stress' – to the whimsical – one of our clients called a particularly bothersome thought pattern 'Gerald'! (Apologies to any Geralds reading this.).

Then, whenever that thought pattern shows up, you can just say, 'Ah, there's Gerald again' (or whatever name you have chosen to give to your thought), without it taking control of you.

This exercise can help you to notice that you are getting stuck to a recurring thought pattern, and to quickly disengage from it. As soon as you have noticed it, you are no longer stuck to it, and when you name it, that reinforces the sense that it is just an event in the mind, and not something that you need to take too seriously.

Exercise 3.8
Not today Mind, thanks
(Adapted from Hayes et al, 1999)

As well as naming specific thought patterns, you can give a name to your mind (or at least the part of it that produces thoughts). You can call it whatever you want: 'Mind', 'Ms Mind', or (of course) 'Gerald'. Then, whenever your mind starts producing thoughts that threaten to take control of you in an unhelpful way, just say, 'Thanks, Mind', to remind yourself that these are just products of your mind. Or you might want to say more. To acknowledge that your mind is, after all, just trying to help you out, you could say something like, 'Thanks, Mind. I know you are trying to help, and I appreciate it, but right now I need to do something different than what you are suggesting'.

This exercise is an extension of the one above: if naming particular thought patterns can help you to step back from those patterns, then naming the mind can help you to step back from any thoughts at all.

Exercise 3.9

I'm having the thought that ...

(Hayes et al, 1999)

When you notice a thought that is liable to pull you off track, simply repeat it to yourself in the form, 'I'm having the thought that ...[insert thought]'. For instance, Rupert in the example above might say to himself, 'I'm having the thought that ... I am in a terrible state and should not go in to work'.

This simple exercise makes it very, very clear that your thoughts are just thoughts. You might find that there is a real difference between just thinking something, and *knowing* that you are thinking it. You might find that when you make it clear to yourself that it is just a thought, it loses some of its power over you. The thought might well come back again, of course – which is no problem at all, as you are not trying to stop the thought but rather to step back from it so that it loses its power. Each time it comes back, just repeat the exercise, as many times as necessary.

Surfing like a pro

Probably some of what we have discussed in this chapter resonates with you, both because it happens to all of us, and because it causes particular trouble in depression. If you are experiencing depression, you might find yourself thinking very intensely, dogged by painful thoughts that you just seem to *know* are the truth, and that have the power to tip your mood downwards in an instant. You might find yourself lost in endless spirals of thought – picking over memories, arguing with yourself, trying to figure out the truth about yourself and your life. Your thoughts might pull so hard on your attention that they almost seem more real and compelling than the world outside; or at least they might take up more of your attention and mental energy. And the upshot of all this might be that you fail to do the things that matter to you, and instead obey the thoughts that say, 'Stay in bed; don't bother trying; it won't work out and will just upset you'.

But it does not have to be this way. Just like the internet, your thinking mind is a tool that can help you move towards the kind of life you want, if you can use it wisely. And just like surfing, you can learn to ride the waves of your mind with grace and skill. There is no need to struggle against your mind or get into arguments with it; your mind is fine just as it is. The challenge is to become aware of your thoughts and to hold them lightly; to take them as suggestions rather than as truths or commands. The ideas and techniques that we have presented in this chapter can help you to begin to do that.

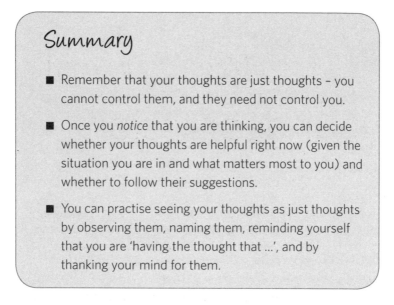

Summary

- Remember that your thoughts are just thoughts – you cannot control them, and they need not control you.

- Once you *notice* that you are thinking, you can decide whether your thoughts are helpful right now (given the situation you are in and what matters most to you) and whether to follow their suggestions.

- You can practise seeing your thoughts as just thoughts by observing them, naming them, reminding yourself that you are 'having the thought that ...', and by thanking your mind for them.

4 You are not your depression

As we noted in the last chapter, our minds are always working, throwing up an endless stream of thoughts. We think about many things: the past, the future, other people, the world. We plan, we worry, we analyse, we wonder. But there is one theme that appears more than any other in our thinking: *ourselves*. We analyse our personalities, our histories, our prospects. We fantasise about the things that we might do, or might have done in the past if things had been different. We imagine what others think of us. Our thinking is endlessly self-referential: all roads lead back to *us*.

In this chapter, we will look at what all this self-focused thinking adds up to, what its consequences are, and how we might step outside it and see ourselves differently. We are going to explore the stories that we tell about ourselves, and who we might be if we look beyond them.

The self-story

If we were to ask you to describe yourself, you might say something like, 'My name is A and I am B years old. I live in C. I'm usually quite a D person, but I've not been feeling myself lately. I think it's because of problems to do with my E – I don't feel like it's really working. I've always been a bit F, which I think goes back to my childhood. My mother was quite a G person. And because of all this I find it hard to do H and I certainly cannot do I.' You would tell us a *story* about yourself – one that is knitted together from your thoughts about yourself, and that has been repeated so often that it has come to seem like *the truth*.

Everyone tells such a story, and these stories certainly have their uses. We have a natural desire for things to make sense, and so it helps if both we and others have coherent stories that render us explicable and predictable. And our own story lets us present ourselves in a particular way to others. But, as with any pattern of thought, holding on too tightly to your story can become constraining and unhelpful, particularly, as is often the case in depression, if it is powerfully negative.

If you are suffering with depression, your story may tell you profoundly unhelpful things about what you can and cannot do; it might be a powerful force keeping you away from the life that you want to live. Even a positive self-story can become a problem, and put us at risk of depression, if we cling to it too tightly. We might stick narrowly to the things that we are good at, and find our lives becoming repetitive and meaningless; or we might struggle to cope when we cannot measure up to our image of ourselves. Any self-story, if we treat it as the last word in who we are and what we can do, limits our flexibility and freedom of action, and that is a recipe for depression.

Yes, you too

Sure, you might say, that sounds reasonable in principle, but *my* story is true. And you would no doubt offer us all kinds of evidence. But this is just how our minds work: we have a natural tendency to notice and remember things that are consistent with what we already think. We like things to be coherent and familiar, and our stories, in a perverse way, make us feel safe: it might, for example, feel safer to believe that you are un-loveable and give up on finding intimacy, than to seek it out and risk the pain of rejection. So, if you suffer with depression, it is likely that you have an eagle eye and photographic memory for anything that seems to confirm your negative view of yourself; and you may be more afraid of giving up that view than you realise.

With the following exercise, you can start to become aware of your story.

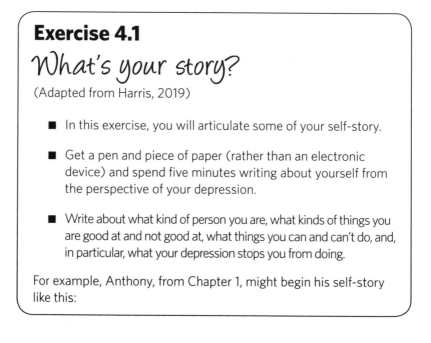

Exercise 4.1

What's your story?

(Adapted from Harris, 2019)

- In this exercise, you will articulate some of your self-story.

- Get a pen and piece of paper (rather than an electronic device) and spend five minutes writing about yourself from the perspective of your depression.

- Write about what kind of person you are, what kinds of things you are good at and not good at, what things you can and can't do, and, in particular, what your depression stops you from doing.

For example, Anthony, from Chapter 1, might begin his self-story like this:

'My name is Anthony and I am 21 years old. I have never been that popular, which is because I am kind of boring. I manage to cover it up by working out what other people are interested in and then talking to them about that, but they usually realise after a while. Because of that, my relationships don't usually last long – my girlfriends get bored and they dump me. Or the last one did, anyway. Since I became depressed, it has become impossible for me to meet anyone else – I don't feel like going out, and I have nothing to say when I do, which makes me even more boring. And if I did get another girlfriend, she'd just find out how boring I am and dump me anyway.'

We aren't going to get into a debate with you about how true your story is or is not. Instead, we invite you to consider whether it is workable. In other words:

- What do you *do* or *not do* when you are in the grip of this story?
- And does that help you move in the directions that you want to go?

For example, when Anthony is in the grip of his story, he wants to disengage from socialising, get into bed, and distract himself with social media. This keeps him safe from the risk of rejection if he were to socialise; but at what cost? His life shrinks, and he is cut off from the very thing that he wants most – connection.

If, like Anthony, your self-story is getting in your way, then we invite you to hold it more lightly, and to see that it is just a story, one that exists within your awareness and that does not have to dictate what you do or don't do. With the next exercise, you can start to practise doing that.

Exercise 4.2

That's my story

(Adapted from Harris, 2019)

- Give your story a name. It can be anything you like. For example, 'The I'm not good enough story; or 'The I'll be alone forever story'. *Anthony called his 'The boring story'.*

- Turn over the page on which you wrote your story, and write, 'This is my [insert name of story] story'.

- Turn back to the story itself and read it. Focus intensely on it – let it pull you in and convince you.

- Then turn the page over again, read the name of your story, and remind yourself of what it is: a story, produced by your mind. You could even acknowledge that your story is trying to help you, but tell it, 'Thank you, Story, but not now'.

Perhaps in doing this exercise you saw a little more clearly that your story *is a story* – one of many that your mind produces. Perhaps, in stepping back from your story, you saw that it need not control you, and that you can step back from it at any time.

You could write down your story and its name, perhaps on your mobile phone, and whenever it dominates your thinking and threatens to take control of your actions, repeat the exercise above. Or you could carry your story in your pocket while you go and do the very thing that it says you should not or cannot do. For Anthony, this meant taking his story with him as he went to a party and sought to connect with others. He realised that if he could do this even with his story in his pocket, then perhaps the story did not have to control him after all.

Beyond the story

There is an alternative to seeing yourself through the lens of your story, and it is one that our clients sometimes discover for themselves in the course of learning to step back from their thoughts. Sometimes, as they practise looking *at* thoughts rather than *through* them, they realise that *we are not our thoughts*. This can be a surprise. We spend so much time glued to our thoughts that they seem to speak with our voice – we identify with them. But if we can be *aware* of our thoughts then we can't also *be* our thoughts. We must somehow be more than our thoughts. And so, every once in a while, one of our clients will say to us, wonderingly, 'But if I'm not my thoughts, then who am I?' This is a very good question indeed.

Exercise 4.3
Who's noticing?

- Take a few moments to notice what's going on right now. Notice what you can see. Notice what you can hear. Notice how your body feels. Notice how you are feeling emotionally. Now notice your thoughts, passing through your mind.

- Ask yourself, 'Who's noticing?' You might have the thought, 'I'm noticing'. But that was just another thought. Who noticed it?

Don't worry, we don't expect you to have an answer to this question, except that *someone* is noticing, and that someone is *you*. As well as being made up of your thoughts, feelings and so on, there is a part of you that notices them. We could call this *awareness*. And just as we often identify with our thoughts – we feel as though the voice in our heads is *us* talking – it is possible to identify instead with the awareness that notices them. Instead of being your thoughts, you can be the awareness that contains them, along with everything else that you are aware of.

Awareness

Let's consider some of the qualities of awareness.

Awareness is big

If awareness contains all the things that you are aware of, then it must be bigger than all of them. Which must mean that *you* are bigger than all of them, and bigger than your depression.

Awareness does not change

Everything that we are aware of changes. Our thoughts change as fast as the streams of data on the internet; our feelings change more slowly but never stand still. What you see, hear, smell and feel changes in every moment. But what about the awareness that is *you*? It never changes, because it has no content – it is the context in which thoughts, feelings and everything else take place.

Awareness is universal

Just as you have awareness, so does everyone else. And everyone's awareness is the same: expansive, open and unchanging. Their thoughts and feelings move through this awareness, just as yours do.

Awareness has always been there

Think back through your life. As far back as you can remember, you have thought things and felt things. You have seen things, heard things and smelt things. You were aware of those things. And so awareness must always have been there. It was always there, and it is here right now. Awareness is the *you* that is stable and constant across time and place.

Let's take a moment to experience this.

Exercise 4.4
Unchanging awareness
(Adapted from Hayes et al., 1999)

- Take up a comfortable position and either close your eyes or lower your gaze.

- Tune into the sensations of breathing and spend a minute or two gently attending to them.

- When you are ready, bring to mind a somewhat painful memory from your childhood. Note that it should only be 'somewhat' painful – don't go for the worst thing that you can remember.

- Try to remember the thoughts and feelings that you had at the time. Notice also the sights, sounds and smells in the memory.

- Notice that if you can notice these things, then you cannot be them. Notice that the part of you that notices them does not change, and never has – it is the same today as it was back then.

- Now, think of a somewhat painful memory from the more recent past.

- Again, recall your thoughts and feelings in the memory, and the sights, sounds and smells.

- Notice that you are more than those experiences – you are the faculty of awareness that noticed them then and notices them now. Notice that this awareness – the *you* that notices – has not changed.

- Now notice your thoughts and feelings in this moment, and the sounds and smells around you. Again, notice that if you can notice these things then you cannot be them. Notice that you are aware of them, and that this is the same awareness that you have had all your life. Notice that it does not change, no matter what passes through it.

Why it matters

We have already seen the usefulness of present-moment awareness and stepping back from thoughts. But there is something special to be gained from seeing that, not only are you capable of awareness, but *awareness is who you are*.

From the perspective of awareness, your thoughts do not define you and they cannot limit or harm you. Awareness is like the sky, and your thoughts and feelings are like the clouds and weather patterns that come and go. Often we lose sight of the blue sky that lies behind the clouds, but the sky remains, untouched by even the fiercest storms, and is spacious enough to contain them.

And if you are awareness, as large and constant as the sky, wouldn't that be good? Might it not offer stability and a broader view in the face of tumultuous moods and the deluge of thoughts? Wouldn't it mean that you are not the narrow version of yourself that your thoughts say you are, and that you are more than your depression? Awareness is always there, if only we are willing to notice it, and it can always be our refuge. From the perspective of awareness, it is possible to stay steady in the face of difficulties, to see what you are capable of, and to choose wisely, in line with the things that matter.

And there is one more thing: when you are awareness, you need never feel alone. Because everyone else has an awareness that is just like yours; that contains their thoughts and feelings but is unchanged by them – the weather differs from place to place, but the sky behind it is always the same. So when your thoughts and feelings tell you that you are alone, that no one else feels this way or has a life as bad as yours, remember who you really are: the awareness that knows these thoughts and feelings. And so is everyone else.

Exercise 4.5
The sky

- If you can, go to a window and look out. Look up at the sky. If you can't do this, bring to mind an image of the sky.

- Notice everything that you can see in the sky – clouds, planes, birds and so on. These are like your thoughts and feelings.

- Now notice the sky itself. Notice how it contains everything within it. The sky is always there and it never changes, though the clouds, planes and birds change constantly.

- Now find a seat and sit comfortably. Close your eyes or lower your gaze. See if you can notice what is passing through your awareness. Notice thoughts, feelings and sounds.

- Notice the awareness that notices these things, and notice that it is larger than than them and does not change. Acknowledge that this awareness is *you*.

As with previous exercises of this kind, you might have found yourself getting lost in thought from time to time. That is fine –

thoughts will never stop, and you will never stop getting lost in them. But perhaps there were moments when you were simply *aware* of your thoughts, your feelings and any sounds that you could hear. And perhaps you had some sense of being that awareness – an awareness that is bigger than what it contains, and unchanging like the sky. You can practise this exercise often, as a way of training yourself to connect with your awareness.

When you need to connect quickly with the perspective of awareness, try the following exercise.

Exercise 4.6
Who?

When you find yourself gripped by a strong emotion or a troublesome thought pattern, for example sadness or worry, simply ask yourself this question:

'Who's sad/worrying (or whatever the feeling or thought pattern may be) right now?'

This can often be enough to remind you that you are bigger than your mental states, and that awareness itself cannot be sad or worried.

You are bigger than your story

You have a choice about who to be. You can look at the world through your thoughts and through your story about yourself, and you can be defined and limited by that story. Or you can be the awareness that contains the story. You can be a small, narrow and rigid self, or you can be wide open, an awareness that is able to accommodate whatever thoughts and feelings pass through you, without being defined by any of them or needing to reject any of them.

When we are able to see beyond our stories about ourselves and adopt the perspective of awareness, we can find stability, strength and clarity. It is from this perspective that we are able to notice and observe our thoughts and feelings, to allow them to come and go, and to freely choose how to respond to them. Unconstrained by our thoughts or the desire to have only good feelings, we are free to notice what we truly want in any given moment, and to move towards it.

Summary

- Remember that your story about yourself is just a story.

- Your self-story can limit you and keep you from doing the things that you want to, which can keep you trapped in depression.

- You are more than your story about yourself, and more than your thinking mind: you are the awareness that contains and notices all of your experiences.

- This awareness is bigger than what it contains, it always remains the same, it is the same for everyone, it has always been with you, and it always will be.

- If you can remember to take the perspective of awareness, rather than that of your story about yourself, you can find the stability, clarity, freedom and wisdom to create the life that you want.

5 Getting better at feeling

Depression feels awful. If you are suffering from depression, then you probably want more than anything to feel better, and that may be the main reason that you are reading this book. But, as we shall see in this chapter, it is precisely our habit of turning away from our feelings – of struggling with and avoiding them – that can lead us into and keep us in depression. In this chapter, we will show you a different way of relating to your feelings: we will show you how to *turn towards* them with an attitude of curiosity and care, so that you can take them with you on your journey towards the life that you want. We invite you to stop trying to *feel better*, and instead to *get better at feeling*.

Exercise 5.1
How life could be

- Imagine that you woke up tomorrow morning and all of your most painful feelings were gone, just like that.

- What would you do? What would become possible if you no longer had to keep bad feelings at bay? Perhaps you would see friends more, or get in shape, or take up a hobby. Perhaps you would go on holiday, or even just for a walk.

- Now ask yourself: what if you could do all of those things *now*? What if the only catch was that you would continue to have your painful feelings, and would need to let them come along for the ride as you do the things that you want to?

Huh?

This might all sound wildly unappealing, or just strange. Our instinct is to run from pain and towards pleasure, and we are bombarded with cultural messages telling us that we should be happy; that we could be happy all the time if only we could get things set up just right. But that is not how our minds work. We are not built for lasting happiness – pain will always arise as we pursue the things that we care about; and we can create it with nothing more than a thought. Pain is an inevitable part of a life well-lived, so if we seek to turn away from it whenever it arises, we will turn away from much of what gives our lives meaning. And then the ordinary, healthy pains of life can become the suffering of depression.

Pain versus suffering

Pain is ... painful. But there is another layer of distress that comes not from the pain itself but from our reaction to it – we can call this layer *suffering*. Say we experience pain because of the end of a relationship. It hurts. That cannot be avoided. It will pass, and it is a necessary part of looking for a relationship that will work for the long term, but it is painful and so we try to get away from it. We ruminate, trying to think our way out of the pain, but that only makes it worse. We feel ashamed of how upset we are, and angry that we feel this way. We feel angry with the pain itself. We drink alcohol and overeat in order to avoid the pain. And we avoid future opportunities to seek out and start a new relationship. After a while, life is not the way we would like it to be, we are suffering intensely, and we seek treatment for depression.

In this instance, the *pain* of the breakup could not be avoided – it is part of the entry fee for a fulfilling life. But that is not true of the *suffering* that followed – the distress that came from our efforts to escape or resist the pain. Pain, we could say, is inevitable, whereas suffering is optional.

Suffering and thinking

The problem for us, as usual, is our clever thinking minds – or rather our tendency to believe them and follow their commands blindly. As we have said in previous chapters, our thoughts can trigger painful feelings even when there is no external threat to us, and they endlessly suggest ways to avoid pain, as though we could get away from it altogether if only we would do what they tell us. So in the aftermath of breaking up with a partner, for example, we might experience not only the natural pain of loss or rejection, but also additional layers of suffering brought on by imagining the reasons why our partner might have left us, or imagining them with a new partner.

And our clever minds do not stop there – they apply their analysis to *other* situations, as well, judging those situations as similarly likely to lead to painful feelings. For example, Anthony, who we met in Chapters 1 and 4, believes that his girlfriend broke up with him because he is 'boring', and now that view of himself colours all of his social interactions. When he thinks of going to a party, he imagines everyone there finding him boring, and feels pain. His mind suggests how he can avoid this pain: by avoiding the party. Or even by avoiding *all* parties. If he does go to a party and meets someone who he finds attractive, his mind will no doubt have something to say about it: it will remind him of how his last relationship ended, predict that trying to form another one will cause him pain, and warn him off taking any steps in that direction. And, as he follows his mind's suggestions for avoiding pain, his avoidance hardens into a habit. Over time, this habit pulls him into depression.

Long term, short term

It is an unfortunate fact about habits that they are shaped much more by the immediate than the long-term consequences of our actions. If something makes us feel good right now, then we will be inclined to automatically do it again, and it will quickly become a habit. Whereas if the benefits appear further down the line, then it has less effect on our behaviour. This is part of how many addictive behaviours work: chocolate tastes good right now, whereas weight gain happens later, and so chocolate is hard to resist.

Avoiding pain can be a lot like eating chocolate: when we manage to do it, we feel better immediately, and so our brains learn that, the next time that we are faced with a similar situation, we should do the same thing. The costs of our avoidance, meanwhile, usually show up later. And so for Anthony, in the example above, staying home from the party brings immediate relief, whereas the costs of doing so – the slow erosion of his friendships and the loss of opportunities to form new ones – lie in the future. And so the habit of avoidance is formed and strengthened.

We hurt where we care

(Hayes, 2019)

As we can see in Anthony's case, it is an unfortunate irony that the situations that cause us the most pain, and that we are most tempted to avoid, are often those that are most important to us. When we approach the things that we truly care about, there is much to gain but also much to lose, and our minds go into overdrive – analysing, predicting and problem-solving, often generating emotional pain and predicting more to come. So if it is our habit to avoid pain, we will habitually recoil from precisely the situations that matter most to us. And, conversely, if we want to do the things that we care about, we have to be willing to turn towards our pain.

Let's take a more detailed look at how we struggle with our feelings, by returning to Judy, whom we met in Chapter 2.

Judy's husband will be home this evening. She has been thinking about having a talk with him about how difficult things are for her at the moment, and the kind of support that she needs from him. But now that his arrival is drawing closer, she has the awful feeling that she always gets when she thinks about any kind of confrontation. When she pictures his face as he hears what she has to say, she feels her stomach clench and twist and a feeling of panic rise up her chest. It is an awful feeling, and she hates it. When she thinks about the feeling in her stomach, she imagines that she is going to be sick, and the panicky feeling gets worse. She tells herself to stop being a baby, and clenches her stomach, bearing down on the feeling, trying to crush it out of existence, but it doesn't go away. She puts her head in her hands, sighing. She can't talk to him feeling like this, she thinks. It will come out all wrong, and then he'll get angry, and she'll wind up backing down and apologising. And if she feels like this now, how much worse will it be when she actually confronts him? She feels a jolt of shame at her own inability to cope with the situation. She'd best just leave it, she thinks, and with that thought, the feeling eases a little. She is relieved. But then she checks, and finds that the feeling is still there, and feels another surge of anger with herself and this horrible feeling, which makes her stomach twist again. She thinks that she is going to get an ulcer, or stomach cancer, if she keeps on feeling this way all the time. There is no way she can talk to her husband, she decides – it will have to wait until she feels better. Her stomach relaxes somewhat, but now she feels shame and contempt for herself for (as she sees it) being weak. She starts tidying the kitchen busily, thinking that at least she can get *this* done.

In this example, Judy is planning to do something that matters to her: having a conversation with her husband that could improve their home life, which is something that she cares about deeply. But precisely because she cares so much about her marriage and about closeness to others in general, her mind begins to warn her that talking to her husband could result in conflict, or even rejection. She feels panic and anticipates further painful feelings if she goes through with her plan. The panic is bad enough, but then she follows up with hatred for the panic, shame and contempt for herself for feeling it, fears that it could harm her physically, and efforts to physically drive it away. Now she is really struggling with her feelings, really suffering, and her mind suggests to her that she could make all of this go away by just deciding not to speak to her husband after all. Her relief is immediate, and so it strengthens her habit of avoidance. The costs of her avoidance, meanwhile – its impact upon her state of mind and her marriage – lie in the future.

Welcoming feelings

The alternative to struggling with feelings is turning towards them. This means opening up to them, approaching them with care and curiosity, and letting them be as they are, in the knowledge that struggling with them does not help. It does not mean tolerating them with teeth gritted, or giving up and resigning ourselves to them. Rather, it is something that we do actively and willingly, because we want to move towards a better life.

All feelings welcome

So what does this look like in practice? Well, it doesn't *look* like anything, from the outside, because it is not something that anyone else can see – it is something that happens privately, between you and your feelings. Only you will ever know for sure how you are relating to them. As to how we cultivate this new relationship with our feelings, we will need to let go of our usual problem-solving strategy: *thinking*. We might be tempted to try and figure out our feelings – where they came from and what they mean – or to talk ourselves round to a more welcoming attitude to them. But that is liable to lead to rumination and suffering. Instead, we can take a different approach: we can learn to connect with our feelings directly by getting to know them as *bodily* experiences.

Emotions in the body

It is a simple biological fact that our emotions show up in our bodies: muscles tighten, heart rate and breathing patterns change, blood vessels constrict or dilate. And this fact shows up in our language: we say that our hearts leap or sink, that our guts are wrenched and our stomachs turn over, that we catch our breath or are left breathless. Anger and shame burn, whereas happiness is a warm glow; and we feel like we are going to burst with pride. Some people can feel the bodily aspect of emotion very clearly, whereas others can't, but with practice most people can start to notice how their emotions show up in their bodies.

Feeling your emotions in the body offers a way to get to know them without reacting to them impulsively or getting lost in the thoughts that accompany them. When Judy felt fear at the thought of confronting her husband, she was assailed by thoughts about how much she hates the feeling, whether it would get worse, what effect it would have on her behaviour, what it says about her as a person, and what effect it might have on her health. Had she been able to simply feel the sensations of anxiety in her body, with a curious attitude, she might have seen the anxiety more clearly: not as a dangerous problem to be solved, but rather as a familiar pattern of feeling in the body that, while it may not be comfortable, could not harm her, need not pull her off track, and may even tell her something important about her life.

To start to build up awareness of your body and of the emotional feelings within it, try the following exercises.

Exercise 5.2
Feel your body

- Bring awareness to your body.

- Just ... feel your body. You can focus in on the sensations in particular parts of it, or have a broad awareness of the body as a whole.

- Perhaps there are sensations of lightness or heaviness, warmth or coolness, relaxation or tension. Perhaps the sensations are flickering or moving. Whatever sensations there are, just notice them as they come and go.

- When your mind wanders, just bring it back to the sensations of the body.

If you do this many times each day, you might find that your attention naturally starts to rest on your body sensations. You are developing a habit of body awareness.

Exercise 5.3
The body scan

This is a longer, more detailed version of the exercise above. You will need to set aside some dedicated time for it – somewhere between 10 and 40 minutes. To develop really good body awareness, do it every day for a while.

- Get comfortable either sitting or lying – lying down is a popular option. Close your eyes or, if you prefer to leave them open, lower your gaze.

- Bring your attention to some part of your body – you could start with the big toe on your left foot. Notice what you can feel there.

- Explore whatever sensations you can feel there. You might feel the touch of your sock against your toe ... warmth or coolness ... tingling ... or nothing much at all. Just notice whatever is there, with a curious attitude.

- Now do the same for the other toes ... the sole of your foot ... the sides of the foot ... and the top of the foot.

- Move through the whole body in this way. If you want to do the body scan quickly, you might scan larger areas all at once, for example the whole of both feet at once. And when your mind wanders, just bring it gently back to the exercise, without criticising yourself.

When doing the body scan, you might have a range of experiences: you might be surprised by the sensations of some parts of the body, you might not be able to feel other parts at all, your mind might wander a lot, or you might fall asleep. All of these experiences are fine: the exercise is just about feeling whatever there is to be felt, while building up your ability to notice when the mind wanders and redirect your attention. And if you do fall asleep, don't be hard on yourself – perhaps you just need some sleep. Don't worry about whether you are doing it right – just do it!

Exercise 5.4
Emotion in the body

To home in on emotion in the body, try this exercise:

- Notice what mood or emotions you are experiencing right now.

- Now tune into your body. Can you notice how your mood is showing up in the form of body sensations?

- Where in the body do you notice these sensations the most? Perhaps the body feels tense, or relaxed. Perhaps your face is flushed, or your hands are cold, or your shoulders are tight. Perhaps you can feel sensations in your stomach or chest area that have something to do with your emotional state.

- Notice how your thinking mind tries to get involved, perhaps by trying to *think* about your mood.

- Just keep bringing your attention back to the feelings of the body.

If you notice that there is some particular place in your body where you feel your emotions, you might want to take your attention there many times each day, to check in with how you are feeling. In particular, people often feel their emotions in their chest area, stomach, throat or head; but, of course, it may be different for you.

On the other hand, you might not notice any emotional feelings in the body. That is fine – you might not have any strong feelings right now, or you might be someone for whom such feelings are less apparent. If you keep on checking in with the body in this way, you might well feel more over time.

Difficult feelings in the body

Building up consistent awareness of the body is very valuable, and never more so than when our emotions are painful. Here we can use some extra skills to help us open up to and accept our feelings. With practice, as you learn to turn down the volume on your thoughts and get to know the emotional feelings in your body, you might find that they are not as bad as you thought. You might even start to find them … interesting.

Exercise 5.5
Turning towards difficulty
(Adapted from Harris, 2008)

This exercise involves getting in touch with your painful feelings directly, without trying to change them or make them go away. This can be challenging at first, particularly if you feel depressed, as these feelings might be quite strong. So be kind to yourself and go gently. You don't have to dive straight into the most disturbing sensations you can find and, as you will see, you can dial down the intensity at any time by paying attention to neutral sensations in your body, such as those in the hands or feet. And, of course, you can always stop the exercise if you start to feel overwhelmed. The aim is to lean gently into your painful feelings, pushing your limits a little, but not too much all at once. So don't back off too readily, but don't push yourself further than is right for you. And hold in mind why you are doing this in the first place: because you want to move towards the life you want, even if it means some discomfort along the way.

- Sit comfortably, and close your eyes or lower your gaze.

- Focus your attention on a part of your body that feels fairly neutral – perhaps the soles of your feet, or your hands, or your bottom on the seat. You can return your attention here at any point during the exercise if you start to feel overwhelmed.

- Now let go of that focus of attention and call to mind an issue that upsets you a bit. Just a bit, though – don't go for the worst thing in your life. Let this issue come into your mind and spend a few moments thinking about it.

- Now, direct your attention to the body.

- Notice any body sensations that are part of your emotional reaction to this issue. For example, you might notice tightening in your chest, butterflies in your stomach, or warmth in your face.

- Explore one of these sensations with an attitude of curiosity, as if you were a scientist encountering it for the very first time. For example:

- If you were able to draw an outline around the sensation, notice what shape it would take.

- Notice whether the sensation sits at the surface of your body or goes deeper inside.

- What is the temperature of the sensation – does it feel warm or cool?

- How about the weight of the sensation – is it light or heavy?

- If the sensation had a texture, what would that be? Is it smooth or rough?

- Is the sensation moving or changing? Perhaps it is vibrating, or pulsating, or still.

- Notice how you are responding to the sensation. You might want it to go away; you might be trying to suppress it or tightening your muscles around it.

- See if it is possible to just let the sensation be there.

  - You could try relaxing any muscles that you are tensing.

  - You could try breathing into the area where the difficult sensation is, and imagining that with each in-breath you create space within you for the sensation, and with each out-breath you breathe out your resistance to it.

■ You could say to yourself, 'It's okay, let me feel this', or, 'I don't have to like this but it's okay for it to be here', or whatever words help you to connect with an attitude of acceptance.

■ You could remind yourself of why you want to accept this sensation – that you are trying to move towards the things that you truly care about.

■ Notice that there is more to you than this feeling. Notice that the *you* that is noticing it must be separate from and larger than it.

■ When you are ready, open your eyes.

What happened for you as you did this exercise? You might have found that your difficult feeling went away, or changed, or that it stayed exactly the same, or even intensified. Any of those experiences are perfectly good, because the object of the exercise is not to change or get rid of your feelings, but rather to relate to them differently – without judgement or defence.

Hopefully, whatever happened to your painful feeling, you got to know it a bit more directly through your own present-moment experience rather than through the story your thoughts want to tell about it. Perhaps you got a glimpse of what it might mean to just accept the feeling – to let it be there, rather than struggling against it. And perhaps you can imagine a little more easily doing what really matters to you in life with your feelings coming along for the ride. Or perhaps you could not feel anything much at all, or were swept away by your thoughts, or felt overwhelmed and stopped the exercise. That is all fine too – it takes practice to build a new relationship with your feelings.

You can practise this technique regularly, as a way of preparing for when difficult feelings show up, and then you can use it on the go when they do show up – it need not take long. Wherever you are and whatever you are doing, you can move your attention into your body, explore the feelings there, and use the breath or some helpful words to help you cultivate an attitude of acceptance towards your feelings.

Embracing the messenger

We have a natural instinct to avoid pain, but all too often our thinking minds turn it into a problem for us. We conjure pain with our own thoughts, we struggle ineffectively with it, and in trying to avoid it, we avoid many of the things that would make our lives rich and meaningful. We can find ourselves expending all of our energy on avoiding or suppressing our feelings, leaving little for anything else, and in consequence our lives become stripped of meaning and become fertile ground for depression.

The alternative is counterintuitive: we need to *turn towards* our feelings. We need to approach rather than avoid them, to see them clearly rather than through the distorting lens of our thoughts, to allow them to run their course, and to make wise choices about what to do next.

The key to this is the body. If we can learn to inhabit our bodies more fully and to recognise our feelings as passing sensations within the body, we can begin to relate to those feelings differently and reduce their control over us. We can explore them with curiosity, get to know them and accept them. No longer compelled to act rigidly and reflexively to make our painful feelings go away, we can find a new sense of freedom to pursue what really matters to us.

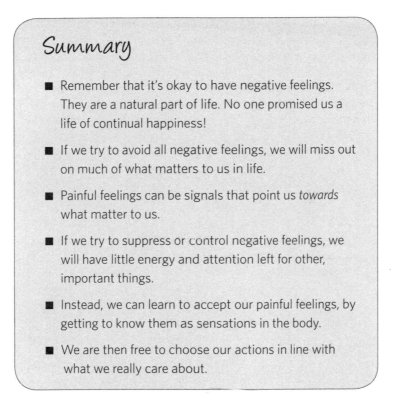

Summary

- Remember that it's okay to have negative feelings. They are a natural part of life. No one promised us a life of continual happiness!

- If we try to avoid all negative feelings, we will miss out on much of what matters to us in life.

- Painful feelings can be signals that point us *towards* what matter to us.

- If we try to suppress or control negative feelings, we will have little energy and attention left for other, important things.

- Instead, we can learn to accept our painful feelings, by getting to know them as sensations in the body.

- We are then free to choose our actions in line with what we really care about.

 Being kind
to yourself

Throughout the preceding chapters, we have encouraged you
to be kind to yourself, and to take a gentle approach to working
with your feelings. This is not just because psychologists are nice,
cuddly people (though we are!), it is because the attitude that you
take to yourself is a key part of the path out of depression. We
want to recommend an attitude of *compassion* towards yourself
and your suffering, including your painful thoughts and feelings.
This is a skill that can be learned and can be woven into your
practice of all the other skills covered in this book. In this chapter,
we will explore what compassion is, why it is helpful, and how you
can start to cultivate it.

What compassion is

Compassion can be defined as a concern for suffering – your own or others' – and the wish to relieve it. Or, to put it in everyday terms, it is what happens when you care about someone and they are suffering: you want to help. And so compassion is less a feeling than it is a motivation or an attitude – you don't have to feel any particular way to practise compassion; it is instead about being motivated to take action to relieve suffering.

Compassion asks us to acknowledge suffering

We cannot hope to relieve suffering, whether our own or others', unless we first notice it, and are willing to attend to it rather than habitually recoiling from it. As we saw in the last chapter, avoiding or struggling with painful feelings tends to exacerbate suffering; instead, we need to turn towards them with a compassionate attitude and be willing to fully experience and explore them.

Compassion asks us to look around

Compassion invites us to notice that we are not the only ones who are suffering: we recognise that pain is an inevitable part of life and that this predicament unites us. In whatever way you are suffering right now, you can be sure that many others are going through the same thing. And you can be sure that *everyone* is suffering in their own particular way.

Compassion asks us to stop blaming ourselves

If we see that suffering is part of being human, then we see that we are not to blame for it. None of us asked to be born into this life, with these minds that tie us in knots and these bodies that suffer ageing, pain and sickness. Nor did any of us choose our parents, or many of the situations that we have found ourselves in. And so we cannot blame ourselves for the suffering that results.

Compassion asks us to take responsibility

While compassion absolves us of blame for our suffering, it asks us to take responsibility for relieving it. Because what happens next is up to us. While we are all in this mess together, it is up to each of us to do what we can to improve it.

Compassion asks us to take action

Compassion isn't just about having a compassionate frame of mind; it is about taking action to relieve suffering. Otherwise it cannot have much effect on us or anyone else. And acting in line with what truly matters to you is always compassionate, because it is the surest way to relieve your suffering.

What compassion is not

Sometimes our clients worry that compassion is weak, or self-indulgent, or will make them lazy. Nothing could be further from the truth. We practise compassion not to sit around feeling good, but in order to take meaningful action in the world, because that is the way to relieve suffering. And while sometimes compassion means being gentle and kind, at other times the relief of suffering will require tougher qualities. To acknowledge and turn towards painful feelings takes courage. To work towards the greatest possible wellbeing takes resolve. And sometimes, when we are faced with injustice or mistreatment, either of ourselves or someone else, we might need courage, resolve and even fierceness: a willingness to fight for the relief of suffering. If we think of some well-known people who have worked hard to end suffering – figures such as Martin Luther King, Gandhi and Mother Teresa spring to mind – we can see that they were strong and courageous, as well as kind.

Why practise compassion?

The need for compassion runs deep in our bodies and minds, because it is a part of our evolutionary heritage. We hug each other, comfort each other and look after each other during times of difficulty, because doing so helped our ancestors to survive.

Think of those ancestors in our distant, cave-dwelling past: they lived in close-knit groups, and none of them could have survived alone. Their children (like ours) were helpless and needed years of care. And so those of our ancestors that formed close, supportive bonds, and who devoted themselves to their children, survived and left behind more descendants than those who did not. And so their distant descendants – us – have inherited the psychological machinery that enabled them to bond with and support one another: feelings and motivations having to do with love, affection, kindness and, of course, compassion.

After hundreds of millennia in which care was central to our lives, we cannot easily do without it. Compassion can help us to meet the challenges that we will face in our journey out of depression and will keep us moving in the directions that matter to us. When we connect with an attitude of compassion towards ourselves and others, we find the courage to face what needs to be faced, and to do what needs to be done.

The comforting parent

On the journey out of depression, we will have to face painful feelings. They can even intensify when we start to take action in line with what matters to us, because *we hurt where we care* – we might fear failure or rejection, or feel shame or sadness about how far we are from the life we want. But if we can bring compassion to these feelings, we are like a parent comforting a crying child. When parents do this, their child is able to calm down, to cope with whatever has upset them, and to re-engage with whatever challenging situation made them cry. But what happens if a parent instead reacts to a child's distress coldly, or with anger and criticism? The child stays upset, and even becomes more upset as their parent's anger and criticism triggers shame, fear or anger of their own. If we want to be able to cope with our pain and keep on moving in the directions that we care about, we will do better to meet it with understanding and kindness than with harshness and self-judgement.

The encouraging teacher

Whatever you want to do, motivation matters. This will be true for every step that you need to take to leave your depression behind, including reading this book and applying the skills within it. Often, we try to motivate ourselves through self-criticism, like a critical teacher trying to motivate students. This works up to a point, because we will make considerable efforts to avoid criticism; if you know that failure to practise the techniques in this book will trigger a storm of self-criticism, you might be motivated to practise them. But consider the effect that self-criticism has upon you: it makes you feel under threat, just as though someone else were criticising you. This is not a good state in which to learn and try out new things. When we are under threat, we find it hard to think clearly or see things in a balanced way, and we aren't at our most creative. Instead we tend to be narrowly focused upon one thing: getting away from the threat. The whole experience can become so unpleasant that you decide to get away from your self-criticism by giving up altogether. So, if you try to do what matters to you – including perhaps reading this book – with a self-critical attitude, you may not stay the course.

When we are compassionate to ourselves, meanwhile, we are like a teacher who is kind, supportive and encouraging. Have you ever had a teacher like that? What was the effect? When we encounter kindness, we feel safe. We are calm, better able to cope with challenges, less fearful of failure, and more confident in trying new things. It is an ideal state in which to learn, and to face whatever painful feelings show up while we do what matters to us. If we want to move forward in any area of our life, including reading and making use of this book, we will find it easier if we can be a kind and supportive teacher to ourselves.

Let's see what it might be like to replace self-criticism with compassionate encouragement.

Exercise 6.1
What does your teacher say?

■ What are some of the more self-critical things that you say to yourself, for example while trying to read this book and use the skills presented in it? Perhaps things like: 'I'm rubbish at this, I can't do it'; 'I can't do anything right, I'm such a failure'; or 'I'm useless and deserve to be depressed forever'.

■ What effect do these words have on you? Do they make you more or less likely to continue with whatever you are trying to do, such as reading the book and practising the skills presented in it?

■ What, instead, would you say to yourself if you were a kind and supportive teacher, who really cared about you and wanted what was best for you? Perhaps something like: 'It's understandable that you find this challenging, given your situation and what you've been through. It's not your fault. You can do this, but take a break if you need to and then come back to it'.

■ To help you get in touch with your inner 'compassionate teacher', you could think of someone to whom you are kind and supportive – perhaps a good friend, or a child. Think about how you would talk to them, if they were trying something new and finding it difficult. What would you say?

■ Could you say something like that to yourself?

■ Notice what effect these words have on you. How motivated do you feel to continue?

Practising compassion

What would it look like to be compassionate to oneself? Let's have a look at it in action.

Anthony is considering going to a party, although he feels nervous about it. He imagines people ignoring him at the party, and feels his chest tighten; he has the urge to get back into bed. Remembering what he has read about compassion, though, he reminds himself to pause and take note of how he is feeling, and how painful it is. He says to himself 'I feel really upset. I'm afraid.' He tries to take a kindly attitude to the feelings, reminding himself that they are just natural responses to facing a situation that matters to him. He reminds himself that it isn't his fault – this is just how the mind works, and it is understandable that his mind throws up these thoughts and feelings, given the experiences he has had in the past. Other people feel like this too, he remembers, and reflects that probably some other people going to the party tonight have thoughts and feelings like this. He feels that he is not alone with this and wishes those people well. And if he wishes them well, he thinks, shouldn't he wish himself well, too? He asks himself what would be the kindest thing that he could do for himself right now. What would he do if he really cared about himself, more than he cares about fitting in, doing what's expected of him, or avoiding pain? He decides that if he really cared about himself, the best thing would be to sit for a few minutes and do some of the exercises that he has learned for working with his thoughts and feelings, including a compassion exercise, and then go to the party, even if he feels nervous and tempted to just lie in bed. He does the exercises, and then he gets ready for the party, and leaves.

Here Anthony uses compassion to give himself courage to face his feelings and do what matters to him.

Although he feels the urge to get into bed and retreat from his suffering, Anthony instead takes a moment to acknowledge his suffering and reflect upon it. This gives him the chance to respond to it in an intentional way, rather than on autopilot.

Taking a compassionate perspective, Anthony is able to see that his painful thoughts and feelings are only natural, are not his fault, and are probably shared by many others, including some of the people he might see at the party. This short-circuits the shame, the self-blame and the sense of isolation that might otherwise compound his fear and make it even harder for him to go to the party.

Recognising that others might be feeling the same as he does, Anthony wishes them well, and in doing so he sees that he too deserves compassion.

Connecting with a sincere motivation to relieve his own suffering, Anthony is able to see clearly what will help him in this moment. He engages in some exercises for working with his thoughts and feelings, and so finds the resolve to do what matters to him: to go to the party.

Now let's try out some exercises for developing compassion.

Exercise 6.2

Compassion for yourself and others

In this exercise, you begin to cultivate compassion for a good friend, and then for yourself. You could do this in two separate exercises, but many people find it easier to direct compassion towards others than towards themselves, and so it can be helpful to first focus your compassion on someone else, and then try to turn it towards yourself. But feel free to experiment.

■ Sit comfortably, with either your eyes closed or your gaze lowered.

■ Tune in to the sensations of breathing, either at the stomach or at the chest, and attend to them gently for a minute or two.

■ When you feel ready, call to mind someone towards whom you feel warm in a fairly straightforward way. A good friend, perhaps, or a niece or nephew. Not someone for whom your feelings are complicated. You could even use a pet.

- Notice how it feels to hold them in mind. Do any feelings show up in the body, perhaps in the stomach or the chest?

- Now begin, very gently and without trying to force anything, to send good wishes to that person (or animal) – a wish for them to be well and not to suffer. You can experiment with different ways of doing this, to find what works for you.

  - You might find it helpful to send them kind words, such as, 'May you be well; may you be free from suffering.' You might synchronise these words with your breathing.

  - You might imagine their smiling face as they receive your compassion.

  - You might imagine a warm golden light shining on them, or compassion flowing from you to them in the form of a warm colour.

  - You can use your imagination here – the aim is simply to find whatever helps you to connect most fully with a wish for this person (or animal) to be well and not to suffer.

- After a few minutes, let this person (or animal) fade from your awareness, and see if you can direct your good wishes towards yourself.

- As before, you can use your imagination. You might say kind words to yourself, or imagine a light shining upon you, or imagine warmth on your skin. You might imagine that you could breathe in kindness and compassion. Whatever works for you. The aim is simply to move very gently in the direction of greater care and concern for yourself and your suffering.

- Continue for as long as feels helpful.

What happened when you did this exercise? Perhaps nothing much. That is absolutely fine – compassion is a marathon, not a sprint, and it is about cultivating positive motivation rather than positive feelings. Remember: we practise compassion to help us take the actions that we want to.

Many people find it easier to cultivate compassion for their friend than for themselves when doing this exercise – you may even have found yourself encountering negative feelings about yourself, and perhaps become upset about those feelings. Again, this is not a problem – it just reveals how much we need to cultivate compassion for ourselves. Keep on practising, taking an accepting and gentle attitude towards your feelings and letting go of any self-criticism for 'not doing it right'.

Exercise 6.3

Receiving compassion

(Adapted from Gilbert, 2010)

In this exercise we begin to cultivate the experience of being cared for by others, so that we can connect with it when we suffer. For this you will need to pick a 'compassionate other' – someone from whom to receive compassion. It would be good to pick someone who has the following qualities: a deep commitment to relieving suffering; the strength to bear your suffering without becoming overwhelmed; the wisdom to understand what you are going through; and a kind, gentle warmth.

If that sounds like a tall order, be reassured that you have a wide field of candidates to choose from. Your compassionate other could be someone you know, someone who is alive but who you have never met, someone who is not currently alive, or someone fictional. It could even be an animal, or some natural feature such a tree or a lake. Be imaginative – you can receive compassion from whoever or whatever you like; but take some time to choose carefully.

- Sit comfortably, with either your eyes closed or your gaze lowered.

- Tune into the sensations of breathing, either at the stomach or at the chest, and attend to them gently for a minute or two.

- When you feel ready, call to mind your compassionate other. Getting a clear visual image is not important – the aim is to allow someone (or something) to care for you, rather than to see them clearly.

- Imagine that your compassionate other truly cares for you, and notice what that feels like. Notice how your body feels.

    - You could imagine the expression on your compassionate other's face as they care for you.

    - You could imagine what caring words they might say, and what tone of voice that they might have. For example, they might say, 'I'm here for you', or 'May you be well'.

    - You could imagine their compassion coming to you in the form of warm light, or a colour that you associate with compassion.

- Play around with different aspects of this imagined experience, to help you get in touch with a sense of receiving compassion.

- Gently explore the sense of receiving compassion for as long as feels helpful.

Again, the most common experience when doing this exercise is of feeling nothing much, and once again that is not a problem, because we are not trying to feel anything in particular, but rather to prepare ourselves for action to relieve our suffering.

When doing this exercise, some people can feel upset. Seeking to connect with the feeling of being cared for might remind you of previous bad experiences with caregivers or others with whom you were close. This is understandable, natural and not a problem. You might want to go gently with the exercise so as not to overwhelm yourself, but getting in touch with the pain of past hurts can often be the first step towards moving on from them. You can apply the technique of *Turning towards difficulty* (Exercise 5.5, *see p101*) to any painful feelings that come up.

Other people might feel upset that the exercise is 'fake' and wish that instead they had a real person in their life to care for them. Again, this is very understandable – it is an expression of the deep need that we all have to be cared for. Just recognising that need can be profoundly helpful, but, more than that, we encourage you to take seriously the value of cultivating feelings of connection even when there is no one around to connect with. After all, most of us have no problem with taking our 'inner critic' seriously – the voice in our heads that expresses all our negative views about ourselves – so why should we not cultivate an 'inner carer' to balance things out?

Exercise 6.4

Pause for compassion

(Adapted from Neff & Germer, 2018)

This is a short exercise that you can do on the go, whenever you need to connect quickly with a sense of compassion for yourself. Try it right now.

■ Pause for a moment, whatever you are doing.

■ If you can, sit comfortably and close your eyes or lower your gaze.

■ Tune into the sensations of breathing.

■ Take a moment to notice and fully acknowledge your suffering.

■ Reflect that you are not alone – that others suffer too.

■ Ask yourself, 'What do I most need to hear right now?', and then offer yourself a few compassionate words of support; perhaps something like, 'May I be kind to myself', 'It's okay to find this hard', or 'You're doing your best'.

You can add a final step to this exercise to turn your compassion into action.

- Ask yourself, 'What compassionate action can I take right now? What would I do if I truly cared about myself?' This action need not be anything grand - it might be as simple as taking a hot bath or having a cup of tea.

- Do it!

A compassionate friend

Depression is defined by suffering, and so compassion – the sincere wish to relieve suffering – must surely be part of the antidote to it. Compassion requires us to face suffering with courage, to see that it is universal and not our fault, and to take appropriate action to alleviate it. If we can do this, we find ourselves able to face our painful feelings and to motivate ourselves with encouragement rather than self-criticism. With stability and courage, we are better able to face challenges, and to keep on moving in the directions in which we want to go. While cultivating compassion can bring up painful feelings and evoke concerns about weakness or self-indulgence, gentle persistence with it can yield great benefits. As always, we ask, 'Does it work?', and encourage you to try it and see.

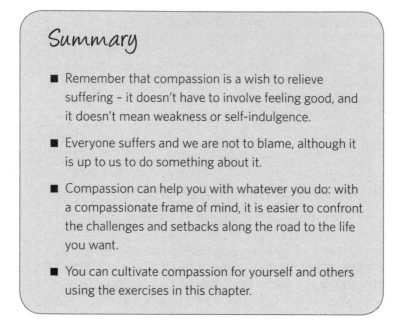

Summary

- Remember that compassion is a wish to relieve suffering – it doesn't have to involve feeling good, and it doesn't mean weakness or self-indulgence.

- Everyone suffers and we are not to blame, although it is up to us to do something about it.

- Compassion can help you with whatever you do: with a compassionate frame of mind, it is easier to confront the challenges and setbacks along the road to the life you want.

- You can cultivate compassion for yourself and others using the exercises in this chapter.

7 The compass and the journey

You have already started moving towards the life you want. You have learned the skills that you need to:

- wake up to the present moment
- step back from thoughts
- be bigger than your depression
- turn towards feelings
- and treat yourself with compassion.

As you continue to practise these skills, you might start to notice a new sense of freedom – the freedom to do what you choose to, instead of what you are compelled to by the force of habit, by the commands issued by your thoughts, and by the urge to avoid painful feelings. In this chapter, we are going to explore how you can make the best use of that freedom – how to decide what it is that you truly want to do, and how to carry your choices into effect. It is time to start taking action.

Why take action?

What you actually *do* with yourself is arguably the most important part of freeing yourself from depression. You will gain far greater satisfaction from doing the things that matter to you than from struggling with your thoughts and feelings, trying to get them in order. That is a fruitless task, as we have seen, because they are not under your control. Your actions, meanwhile, are the one thing that you can control.

Exercise 7.1
Who's in control?

- Try not to think of a pink elephant for 30 seconds.

- Now try to fall in love.

- Now try to raise your arm.

- Which one was easiest?

This is a trivial example, but the point it conveys is important: you cannot control your internal experience – your thoughts and feelings – but what you do in the external world – where you go and what you do, and how you do it – is up to you. You can choose to live according to the rules of depression, avoiding pain even if it means also avoiding what matters to you, or you can choose to live the life that you want, and find meaning and joy along the way.

The importance of compassion

While it is true that you have control over your actions, it is also true that depression can make many things harder to do, so be gentle with yourself. In this chapter, we will encourage you to push the limits of what your mind says you can do, but gently, by starting small and building up to the bigger changes that you want to make in your life. And we suggest that you do it with a compassionate attitude. Encourage yourself as you would a good friend, using the exercises from the previous chapter; and if you fail to do something that you had planned to do, be kind to yourself. And then plan once again to take action.

So what should I do?

There are certain things that are likely to improve most people's lives, simply because we are all human and share the same basic needs. We all need to take care of ourselves by eating well, sleeping well and exercising. And for our lives to feel satisfying and worthwhile, most of us need strong relationships with others, activities that give us a sense of achievement, and opportunities to enjoy ourselves. Again, think of our cave-dwelling forebears: they survived and thrived if they were healthy, got on well with their fellows, tried to excel at useful activities, and took time to relax. So you would do very well indeed to make time for these things, and they can go a long way towards lifting you out of depression. You don't have to do it all at once – day by day, little by little, you can build new, more helpful habits.

But you can go one better: you can identify what it is that *you*, as an individual, truly want; what uplifts you and makes it seem worthwhile to get out of bed in the morning. And then you can take action to move your life in that direction. You can identify, and live by, your *values*. You will still have painful thoughts and feelings, because the human nervous system does not have a 'delete' function, but it will be in the context of a life that has meaning and vitality because it is oriented to what you truly care about.

What are values?

Values are the qualities that you would like to embody in your life. The things that, if you were to look back at your life when you are very old, you would want to have stood for. Examples of values are qualities such as 'determination', or 'kindness', or 'supporting others', but the list is virtually endless (and you can find plenty of lists online). Any quality that could describe you or your actions can be a value. Values are not the same as goals, are freely chosen, and are ends in themselves.

Values are different from goals

A goal is a fixed point that we want to get to, whereas a value is a direction that we want to move in; it's like the difference between 'heading for California', and 'heading West'. When we achieve our goal of getting to California, our job is done and we need to think of another goal to aim at. And if we don't get there, then we have failed, and our efforts have been wasted. Whereas you can always keep moving in the direction of your values: you never get to the end of 'heading West', and nor can you fail to get there. There is always more to do, and a range of ways in which you could do it: if you can't get a flight to California, you could go to New Mexico instead. You will need to set goals in order to serve your values – you will want to aim at various westerly destinations (such as California) along the way – but it is values that can provide a consistent source of meaning and purpose in your life. Values are the compass that guides you on your journey.

Let's apply this idea to the value of 'kindness'. If you want to live by it, you might set a goal of becoming a nurse, so that you can embody it in your work. But when you meet that goal, your work isn't done – now you need to actually be kind as a nurse! And if you don't manage to become a nurse, that is not a problem. You might choose a different job in which you can embody kindness, or you might do some volunteering work, or you might simply try to be kind to whoever crosses your path (including yourself, of course). And, however you decide to embody kindness, it is the process of doing so that will reward you, rather than any particular outcome.

Values are freely chosen

You might have been told by others, or by the wider culture, that you *should* value certain qualities, but that is not the same as truly valuing them. When we try to follow rules that have been set for us by others, we won't be truly satisfied or truly motivated, and sooner or later we will wonder just why we are doing what we are doing. Your values are the qualities that truly move *you*, and make *your* life feel worthwhile.

Values are ends in themselves

We do not live in accordance with our values in order to be liked, accepted or praised. We do it because it is what we *value*, quite apart from what rewards might come our way as a result. We would carry on even if no one else ever knew.

Why live by values?

As we have said at various points in this book, it is natural to want to avoid pain. But it often does not work very well, because our minds trigger painful feelings even when nothing bad is happening, and warn us of the pain that we might encounter if we try to do the things that we want to. Whereas when we orient ourselves not *away* from pain but rather *towards* what is meaningful to us, we can keep on moving in that direction even when painful feelings show up. And when we move towards what is meaningful – what truly matters to us – we find fulfilment that goes beyond short-term happiness or pleasure.

What values should I live by?

The answer, of course, is that only you can decide that. There are no right or wrong values, and each person's values are particular to them, although of course there is a lot of overlap. But watch out – it can be hard to distinguish our own, deeply held values from rules we have picked up from others. And when you are suffering with depression, it can be hard to even think about values. In depression, our lives become constricted and limited, and we may lose touch with our values so completely that we forget what they are, or that we could even have such things. And beginning to think about values can be painful, if we feel that we are very far away from living in accordance with them. In fact, what you value the most might be precisely in the area where you feel the most pain and are most avoidant. If you did not care, it would not hurt so much.

Rupert is at home, sitting in the living room, alone. He feels despondent ... It seems as though his depression has been going on forever and will never end. He doesn't know what to do. He looks over at his guitar in the corner and feels a pang of sadness. Where did it all go? He remembers the years when the band was active, how happy he was. The fun that they would all have together – rehearsing, in the studio, backstage at gigs. The challenge and satisfaction of writing new songs. The sheer ecstasy of playing live – up there on stage sharing all his creativity and joy with an audience. He feels so sad that he had to give it up. But there was so much to do, with work and the kids, and it always ate up more money than it made. It just wasn't sustainable. They all keep in touch, but infrequently, and only Mark is still making music. He texted Rupert a few weeks ago, asking if Rupert could help out with some guitar parts on something he was recording, but Rupert said that it wasn't possible at the moment – the same thing he always says. The sadness intensifies, and Rupert feels himself welling up. How can all of that have gone away? It was the best thing in his life, once upon a time. But it's just not possible, he thinks – it's not worth thinking about now.

In this example, we can see that Rupert has become disconnected from what he truly values in life, and this disconnection has fed his depression. He loved playing in a band; the satisfaction that it gave him had something to do with his relationship with the other band members, the experience of creating music, and the pleasure of sharing it with audiences. So Rupert might, if he thought about it, identify 'comradeship', 'creativity' and 'sharing what I love' as values that are important to him. If he can get past the pain of realising how far he has drifted from these values, and the thoughts that tell him that it has to be this way, then he might start to imagine a future in which he reconnects with them.

Identifying your values

The skills that you have been practising so far in this book can help you to identify your values without becoming snared by your thinking mind or being driven back by a desire to avoid pain.

In daily life, you can start to notice when your values are in play by using present-moment awareness and a sensitivity to emotions in the body (see Chapters 2 and 5). You might notice the joy and satisfaction that comes from connecting with a value; or you might feel the pain that comes from being cut off from your values, as Rupert did in the example above, or from wanting to connect with your values but fearing that it won't work out.

And if, while working on the exercises below or in daily life, your mind tries to get in the way by telling you what you *should* do, or *cannot* do, we hope that you will be able to step back from those thoughts and not be controlled by them (see Chapter 3). If pain arises, we hope that you will be able to turn towards it and keep on with the task of identifying your values (see Chapter 5). And if your mind offers criticism for not living by your values, or perhaps criticism of the whole idea of identifying values, we hope that you will be able to connect with compassion for your predicament and a heartfelt wish to press on, in the interests of relieving your suffering (see Chapter 6).

Before we dive into identifying your values, there are a few points to bear in mind.

Values vary across situations

You will not have the same values in every area of your life. For instance, you might value being romantic in your intimate relationship, while at work you might value being ambitious or diligent.

Values can change

Your values will evolve over time, so there is no need to worry about getting them 'right' first time – you can always change them or come up with new ones for new situations. The idea is to hold them lightly, knowing they might change tomorrow, yet pursue them vigorously today.

Values can conflict

Sometimes two values might point you in opposite directions. Much of the time, this is really about how you prioritise two different areas of your life: being available for your children might conflict with being ambitious at work. At other times, an apparent conflict might not really be one: should you be honest by telling your friend a hard truth, or should you be kind by keeping silent? Well, perhaps it would actually be kindest, in the long run, to tell them, and perhaps there is a way to do it gently. At other times, you might have to choose between two values in the same area of your life. There is no magic formula for doing this – you will ultimately have to decide which one takes priority. But be reassured that conflicts (and apparent conflicts) between your values do not mean that there is a problem with your values. It is fine to prioritise different values at different times. Imagine that your values are like the continents on a spinning globe – as the globe slowly spins through the day, different values come to the front, but those that are at the back of the globe are still there, and will come to the front once again soon enough.

Now, with all of that said, let's begin to clarify your values.

Exercise 7.2

Be a hero

- Ask yourself who you most admire. It could be a famous figure from history, someone who is alive now, or even a fictional character.

- What do you admire about them? Probably, it is not their apparent happiness, but something they do that seems worthwhile. Maybe they help others. Or maybe they show courage in the face of adversity. Or maybe they are conscientious and creative.

- Whatever you admire about them, it is likely that it has something to do with your values. They embody a quality that you value. And in admiring them, you wish to share in that quality.

- List the qualities that you admire in this person – what they stand for and how they live their life.

- Notice how it feels to think about those qualities – do you notice anything in your body? Perhaps you feel excitement or sadness – that might mean that these qualities matter to you; that they are some of your values. Or if you don't feel anything much, that is fine – you can list these qualities as possible values and see how they fit with you over time.

Please note that in doing this exercise, we are not asking you to compare yourself to this person, or to try to achieve whatever it is that they have achieved. Instead, we are asking you to notice what *qualities* you admire in this person; how you go about embodying them will be particular to you and might begin with the smallest of actions. If, for example, you value 'determination', then right now, for you, that might mean something as simple as getting up and going to the shops, rather than trying to emulate the achievements of your heroes. In time, you might move on to grander goals, but you can start living in accordance with your values right away.

Exercise 7.3
Be uplifted
(Adapted from Hayes, 2019)

■ Think of a particularly sweet time in your life, a time when you felt that you were really living the way that you wanted to. It could be as short as a moment, or a much longer period. Perhaps it involved doing something that felt meaningful or worthwhile – something that connected with a grander vision for your life than just seeking pleasure. Perhaps you remember moments with your children, or other family members. Or working hard on something you believed in. Or doing something to help others. These were probably times when you were living out your values.

- Notice how you feel when you remember this time in your life, in particular what sensations show up in your body. That just might be the feeling of connecting with your values.

- Can you identify any values that you were connected with at that time? For example, Rupert, in the example above, remembers the good times he had in his band and could draw from it the values of 'comradeship', 'creativity', and 'sharing what I love'.

Once again, we are not asking you to somehow replicate the joy you experienced in the best moments of your life. We are drawing your attention to them to show the direction in which fulfilment can be found. And you can begin to move in that direction *now*, with whatever smalls steps are possible for you.

Exercise 7.4

Turn pain into purpose
(Adapted from Hayes, 2019)

■ Reflect on where in your life the greatest pain shows up.

■ Ask yourself why it hurts so much. What does it reveal that you care about? Or, to put it another way, what would you need to not care about in order to not feel this pain?

■ Perhaps this points the way to a value. For example, in Chapter 1, Anthony felt great pain when he thought about being rejected by others. If he were to consider why this hurts so much, he might realise that he values connection with others, and that this is something that he needs to pursue.

You can also use this technique on the go, in any moment when your pain shows up. Whatever you are doing, simply pause, connect with present-moment awareness, notice your thoughts and feelings, and ask yourself the questions above. You might just find that a value is calling for your attention.

Exercise 7.5

Take a closer look at your life

(Adapted from Wilson, Sandoz, Kitchen, & Roberts, 2010)

- For each of the following areas of your life, see if you can come up with at least one value.

  - Relationships and family (e.g. 'being supportive', 'patience')

  - Work and education (e.g. 'diligence', 'ambition')

  - Recreation and health (e.g. 'being adventurous', 'being physically active')

- Now think about which other areas of your life you would like to identify values for.

- You might break up the areas listed above into smaller sub-areas. For example, 'relationships and family' could be broken up into 'intimate relationship/marriage', 'birth family', 'parenting', and 'friends'.

- Or you might come up with completely new areas. For example, 'community engagement' or 'spirituality'.

- For each of these areas, come up with at least one value.

We are likely to have different values in different areas of our life, and so, to live the fullest and most purposeful life that we can, we will want to identify our values in as many of those areas as possible. This exercise will help you to do that.

Exercise 7.6
Take stock of your values
(Adapted from Wilson et al., 2010)

For each of the areas of life that you have considered above, ask yourself:

- How important is this area of my life to me? Give the answer as a score of 1–10, where 1 is 'completely unimportant' and 10 is 'very important'.

- How much have I managed to live by my value(s) in this area of life, during the past week? Give the answer as a score of 1–10, where 1 is 'not at all' and 10 is 'totally'.

This exercise can help you decide where to start in reorienting your life towards your values. You might want to start with areas that scored more than five for 'importance' but less than five for 'living by my values', as these are the areas where you can make the biggest difference to your quality of life. But of course, until you are living completely by your values in every area, there is always more that you can do.

In doing this exercise, you might realise that you are quite far from living by your values, and this could trigger self-criticism and emotional pain. If that is the case for you, then we invite you, as always, to be compassionate to yourself. Remember that: you are not alone (in large or small ways, we all deviate from our values every single day); you are not to blame; and kindly encouragement will be more helpful than harsh self-judgement.

Now, let's get ready to start taking *action* in the service of your values.

What actions should I take?

The actions that you take should, of course, be linked to your values. This will involve setting goals, because, as we have said, goals are crucial for living in accordance with values. But it is important to keep in mind that goals are useful because they serve your values, not the other way around.

In a moment we will identify some goals to begin working towards. But first, here are some tips on how to do it.

Start small

Start with goals that feel manageable and actions that can be done *soon*. Achieving small goals will give you the confidence to aim for bigger ones over the longer term. And often these bigger goals can themselves be broken down into a series of smaller steps, each of which can be a less daunting goal in its own right.

'Small and manageable', though, should not mean 'entirely comfortable' – your goals should stretch you, at least a little. Moving towards your values should take you out of your comfort zone, because if the things that you truly want to do were easy, you would probably be doing them already.

Be active

You should plan to *do* things, not to *not* do things. So, 'I will stop eating sweets', could be replaced by 'I will eat fruit when it is time for dessert'.

Be 'SMART'

Your goals should be 'SMART', which stands for:

Specific – If you say, for example, 'I want to develop my career', it is not clear exactly what you are planning to do, and so your plan will be difficult to implement. Whereas if you say, 'I want to go back to university to do a degree in nursing and then become a nurse working with children', then you will know what you need to do to achieve this.

Measurable – You need to be able to measure progress towards your goal. When pursuing the goal, such as the one in the example above, measuring progress will be relatively easy: have you researched possible nursing courses yet? Have you got your application in before the deadline? Have you been accepted onto a course? Are you attending the lectures and getting passing grades for your work? Whereas with a vaguer goal, such as 'I want to develop my career', there is no clear way of measuring progress.

Attainable – Your goals should stretch you, but there is no point in having a plan that you cannot carry out. Planning to win a Nobel Prize for your humanitarian work as a nurse might be setting yourself up to fail.

Relevant – Once again: your plans should relate to your values. Ask yourself regularly, 'Does this plan truly serve one of my values? Or have I become distracted by some sense of what I *should* be doing or what I think will impress others?'

Time-bound – Without a time limit on your goal, it is possible to procrastinate endlessly. If you want to achieve your goals and live according to your values, you will need deadlines.

Now let's practise making plans to achieve your goals, in accordance with your values.

Exercise 7.7
Make a plan

Pick one of your values, and in a table like the one below, outline what you can do to live in accordance with it. Think of where you want to get to over the longer term, and what the steps are that can take you there, bit by bit. And remember to make each goal along the way a SMART goal.

	What can I do to live in accordance with my value in the next ...				
Value	**Year**	**Month**	**Week**	**Day**	**Hour**
E.g. Kindness	Begin a degree in nursing	Apply for a degree in nursing	Choose where to apply for a degree in nursing	Read about different nursing courses	Search online for nursing courses

Just by filling in a table like this, you are taking action that is in line with your values. Notice how that feels - is there any sense of satisfaction or excitement as you do it? As always, don't worry if there isn't, or even if you feel sadness or anxiety - that might be a sign that this course of action matters to you, and that you should keep going with it. The beauty of valued action is that you don't have to wait long for it to pay off, because its effects start the minute you start taking action. Remember: values are about the journey, not the destination.

Doing it

So, now you have a plan, and all you have to do is follow through on it. But of course that is easier said than done - we have all had the experience of making plans, resolutions and even heartfelt promises to ourselves which we then completely fail to hold to. Fortunately, psychologists have built up quite a store of knowledge about how to give ourselves the best chance of doing what we plan to. Here are some tips and techniques:

Full commitment

Whatever you decide to do, we want you to commit fully to doing it, not to *maybe* doing it *if* you feel like it *and* you are sure that it is going to go well. The point is not that your actions should always have the desired outcome – that is impossible – but rather that you take those actions in the first place, in accordance with your values. And you are much less likely to do that if you have given yourself an escape clause. If your plan is to do something that is appropriately small and SMART, then there is no good reason not to commit to it.

To strengthen your commitment, try this:

Tell someone else – We are more likely to carry out our plans when we involve someone else in them. They might be able to help us, encourage us, or even just remind us to do what we intend to. Even if they do no more than hear us out, just having shared our intention with them can help us to follow through on it.

Tell yourself – Saying out loud what you intend to do can have a similar effect to telling someone else.

Tell yourself regularly – You could take a few moments at the start of each day to think of one or more values that you intend to work on that day, and how you intend to do it. Or you could use a written reminder, for example a note in your phone or on the fridge.

Prepare for challenges

It is to be expected that taking action in accordance with your values will be difficult at times – if it were easy, you would be doing it already. Your mind is likely to try to talk you out of it, and all sorts of painful feelings might show up. And of course there will be practical obstacles too. But all of this is not a problem, because you have learned a range of skills for dealing with difficult thoughts and feelings, and many practical problems can be solved. In fact, painful feelings are a good sign: they show that you are moving in the right direction. And challenges of all kinds can be welcomed: they are opportunities to practise your skills for coping with them, and to develop resilience.

It can be helpful to get ready for the challenges that might show up, so let's take a few minutes to think about them, and about what you can do to meet them. You might find that filling in a table such as the one in Exercise 7.8 (*see p154*) is helpful.

Exercise 7.8
Be prepared

What is my goal?	What thoughts might get in my way?	What feelings might get in my way?	What external obstacles might get in my way?	What can I do to meet these challenges?
E.g. Apply for a nursing degree.	'I dropped out of university before; it will probably happen again.' 'If I don't get accepted, then applying will have been a waste of time.'	**Emotions** Boredom, anxiety, shame. **Body sensations** Tiredness.	Application deadlines are soon, and I am busy.	Use the skills I have learned to step back from thoughts and turn towards feelings. Put a note on the bathroom mirror to remind me why I am doing this, i.e. my values. Ask my manager if I can do fewer shifts at work over the next few weeks.

Stay focused on values

When challenges show up, remember why you are doing what you are doing; keep your values in sight, and remember that a life lived according to them will bring you meaning and joy. But avoid getting too focused on the specific goal that you are working towards, as a strong focus on the endpoint of your plan is liable to get in your way – you might become demoralised because it seems too distant or because you encounter setbacks, or you might lose interest. Whereas if you remember what values are being served by your actions – what qualities you are seeking to embody in every moment of your efforts – it becomes possible to enjoy the process regardless of how near or far you are from your goal.

When you face setbacks

Notice that we say '*when*', not '*if*', you face setbacks. This is because setbacks are inevitable! No one ever did anything worthwhile without some false starts and wrong turns. It is how you respond to them that determines how effective your actions will be.

There is much to be learned from setbacks. By failing, you can learn what you need to succeed next time. By trying again, you can develop confidence in your own resilience. And in coping with the painful thoughts and feelings that inevitably accompany setbacks, you can practise all of the skills that you have learned in this book. You might even reflect on what values you want to embody when you face setbacks; for example, 'persistence', 'compassion' or 'good humour'.

In any case, if you remain focused on your values, success or failure in achieving particular goals is not really the point – the point is to act in accordance with your values. And that you can always do, even in the face of setbacks. You can simply recommit to your values, and act in accordance with them in the next moment, and the next.

What are you waiting for?

Rupert has been thinking about the band again. He has been reading a book about depression and using some of the techniques in it. He is not so sure now that it is 'not possible' for him to make music. He still feels sad when he thinks about it, and also scared of trying to get back into it after all these years, and his mind is throwing up lots of reasons why it wouldn't be a good idea. But now he understands that perhaps that need not stop him doing it. He has been thinking about what he could do, but he is not really sure yet. He can't restart the band and go on tour again, but there must be *something* he could do. Mark texted him yesterday, just to say hello. Maybe talking to Mark would lead somewhere, although he doesn't know quite where. It seems like just doing that could be a small step in the right direction, and when he thinks of making the call, he feels excited. He feels scared and sad too, but there is an excitement that seems to come from deeper down - it feels like the direction he wants to go in. He picks up his phone.

In the example above, Rupert begins the process of taking action in accordance with his values. He doesn't have a clear plan yet – that can come later. But he knows that there is no time like the present – it is never too soon to start living according to your values. So ask yourself: is there something that you can do *right now*, no matter how small, that would be in accordance with one of your values? There almost certainly is. And so we invite you … to do it!

Following your compass

Depression is ultimately a problem of moving in the wrong directions: we lose sight of the kind of life we truly want and the sort of person we truly want to be, and we stop moving towards these aspirations. We lose touch with what we care about, and the meaning and vitality drains out of our lives. The way to get it back is not to struggle with our thoughts and feelings, but rather to take action in accordance with our *values*. Values are personal to each one of us, freely chosen, and are distinct from goals in that they describe directions that we want to go in rather than destinations that we want to get to – which means that it is always possible to take action in accordance with your values, and in a range of ways.

To move in the direction of values means, of course, taking action. We do not have to do everything at once – it is wise to start small – but there is no reason to delay. Our actions are the one thing that we can take control of, and we can start to do so today. But we will need a plan, preferably setting out a sequence of goals that are **s**pecific, **m**easurable, **a**ttainable, **r**elevant and **t**ime-bound. To give ourselves the best chance of achieving our goals, we can use a range of techniques to maximise our commitment, overcome challenges, stay focused on values, and keep on going even when we face setbacks.

And throughout this process, we will need to use the skill of compassion. It can be painful at first to think about our values and how far we might have drifted from them, and it can be challenging to take action in their service, especially when things don't go as planned. And so we hope that you will remember at every stage of the process that there is no need for self-blame, that others suffer just as you do, and that the best way to motivate yourself is with kindly encouragement, not self-criticism and self-blame.

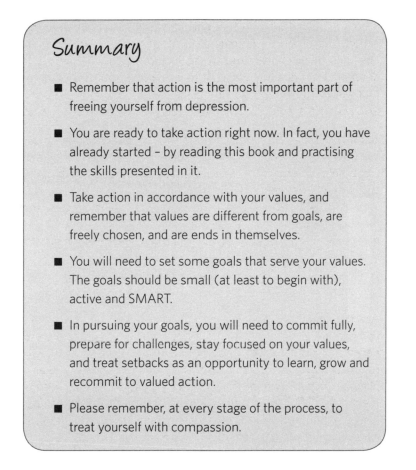

Summary

■ Remember that action is the most important part of freeing yourself from depression.

■ You are ready to take action right now. In fact, you have already started – by reading this book and practising the skills presented in it.

■ Take action in accordance with your values, and remember that values are different from goals, are freely chosen, and are ends in themselves.

■ You will need to set some goals that serve your values. The goals should be small (at least to begin with), active and SMART.

■ In pursuing your goals, you will need to commit fully, prepare for challenges, stay focused on your values, and treat setbacks as an opportunity to learn, grow and recommit to valued action.

■ Please remember, at every stage of the process, to treat yourself with compassion.

8 Moving forwards

Although this is the end of the book, it is the beginning of your journey towards the life that you want. In reading this book and learning the skills presented within it, you have taken an important step, but the skills that you have learned will benefit you only to the extent that you practise them. In this final chapter we will show you how all the skills fit together, give you some tools to help you use them when you need them, and offer some advice on responding to the downs that accompany the ups on the road out of depression.

In Chapter 1 we laid out four processes that underlie depression:

- losing touch with the here-and-now
- struggling with thoughts and feelings
- being harsh and self-critical
- not doing what matters.

In Chapters 2 to 7, we introduced you to the skills that you need to reduce the impact of these processes upon your quality of life:

- present-moment awareness and flexible attention (Chapter 2)
- stepping back from thoughts (Chapter 3)
- being more than the story that your mind tells about you (Chapter 4)
- turning towards your feelings (Chapter 5)
- being compassionate (Chapter 6)
- clarifying values, and acting in accordance with values (Chapter 7).

Tying it all together

These skills are not really separate, rather they depend upon and reinforce one another. As you become more familiar with them, you will find yourself weaving them together intuitively to meet the demands of the moment. Recall the analogy of playing a sport: to do it well, you need good fitness, muscular strength and control, the right attitude, a good grasp of tactics ... and probably much more. These skills and attributes often depend upon and support one another, and the skilled sportsperson, over time and with practice, learns to use all of them together, without needing to stop to think about which skill or attribute is needed in any given moment. Your use of the skills offered here can be the same, with time and practice. Let's take a closer look at how they can fit together, by returning to Judy, who we met in previous chapters.

Judy's husband is home, and she is planning to talk to him. The last time she planned to, she ended up not doing it, and then spent most of the next day in bed, going over and over things in her mind, criticising herself for her weakness, and alternately hating and trying not to hate her husband.

Having practised some of the techniques she'd been learning about, however, she saw more clearly what was going on (*present-moment awareness and flexible attention*). She saw that backing away from conflict with her husband had made things worse, not better – something she had not noticed before. Since then, she has spent some time figuring out what she really wants out of her family life (*clarifying values*) – closeness to her husband, but also self-respect and honesty – and this morning at the start of her mindful breathing exercise, which she does every morning now (*present-moment awareness and flexible attention, stepping back from thoughts*), she committed to having a talk with her husband (*acting in accordance with values*).

Inevitably, Judy's mind is trying to talk her out of it: she keeps having thoughts about this not being the right time, and about the consequences if the talk turns into an argument. But she just notices these thoughts, and her body tensing in response to them, and that there is an urge to stay silent and let the evening go on as usual (present-moment awareness and flexible attention, stepping back from thoughts, turning towards feelings). She reminds herself of what matters to her in this situation (clarifying values), however, and thanks her mind for trying to help her by warning of possible dangers, but reassures it that she knows what she is doing (being more than the story, stepping back from thoughts). Her mind keeps on telling her that she can't do this – that she is no good with conflict and will be even more depressed if there is an argument – and for a few moments she is pulled into this train of thought. But she notices what is happening (present-moment awareness and flexible attention), and she thinks that this is just her story about herself (being more than the story, stepping back from thoughts), and notices instead that she is aware of the story in her mind, and so is larger than the story and need not be controlled by it (being more than the story).

She can hear her husband coming down the stairs now, and she feels a stab of panic, and her mind starts to race. But she

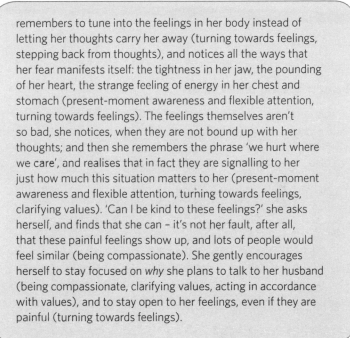

remembers to tune into the feelings in her body instead of letting her thoughts carry her away (turning towards feelings, stepping back from thoughts), and notices all the ways that her fear manifests itself: the tightness in her jaw, the pounding of her heart, the strange feeling of energy in her chest and stomach (present-moment awareness and flexible attention, turning towards feelings). The feelings themselves aren't so bad, she notices, when they are not bound up with her thoughts; and then she remembers the phrase 'we hurt where we care', and realises that in fact they are signalling to her just how much this situation matters to her (present-moment awareness and flexible attention, turning towards feelings, clarifying values). 'Can I be kind to these feelings?' she asks herself, and finds that she can – it's not her fault, after all, that these painful feelings show up, and lots of people would feel similar (being compassionate). She gently encourages herself to stay focused on *why* she plans to talk to her husband (being compassionate, clarifying values, acting in accordance with values), and to stay open to her feelings, even if they are painful (turning towards feelings).

Using the skills that she has learned, Judy is ready to do something new, and move towards being the person she wants to be. It does not stop there, of course – Judy's habitual patterns of behaviour will try to reassert themselves repeatedly, and she will need to continue using her new skills to stop that happening. But over time, as she continues to practise and use her new skills, they can become new habits that manifest themselves readily when needed.

Remembering what to do

For you, as for Judy, using these new skills can, with practice, become second nature. A neat way to apply them whenever you find yourself in a challenging situation is to ask yourself the following questions (Adapted from Polk, Schoendorff, Webster & Olaz, 2016).

- What can I notice right now outside myself (e.g. sights, sounds, etc)?
- What can I notice right now inside myself (e.g. thoughts, self-story, emotions, sensations)?
- What would I do if I let these thoughts and feelings control me?
- What matters to me in this situation? What are my values?
- What would I do if I acted in line with these values instead – if I acted like the person I want to be in this situation?
- How can I be kind to myself in this moment, as I take this values-led action?

In order to build the habit of using these questions, it is of course helpful to start practising *now*, in situations that are not particularly challenging. If you practise using the questions regularly – at least three times per day, say – then you are more likely to use them when you really need them.

You can even strengthen this new habit by using your imagination: simply imagine challenging situations from the past, or ones coming up in the future, and explore them through the lens of the questions above. Each time you do this, you make it easier to do it the next time. Let's try it.

Exercise 8.1
Notice, and take action

- Take up a comfortable position and either close your eyes or lower your gaze.

- Tune into the sensations of breathing and spend a minute or two gently attending to them.

- When you are ready, call to mind a challenging situation from the past or future in which you would like, or would have liked, to use your new skills. Imagine it as vividly as you can.

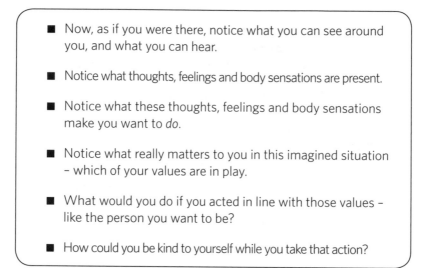

- Now, as if you were there, notice what you can see around you, and what you can hear.

- Notice what thoughts, feelings and body sensations are present.

- Notice what these thoughts, feelings and body sensations make you want to *do*.

- Notice what really matters to you in this imagined situation – which of your values are in play.

- What would you do if you acted in line with those values – like the person you want to be?

- How could you be kind to yourself while you take that action?

And, finally, in those moments when you need to think fast, you can always turn to the acronym that we introduced you to in Chapter 1, as a quick and easy reminder of the full range of skills that you have learned in this book:

F – *ocus* on what is right here, right now

R – *elease* your struggle with thoughts and feelings

E – *ncourage* yourself with a kindly attitude

E – *ngage* in action according to what matters to you.

Again, practise using this acronym often – each time you look at a situation through the lens of **FREE** or the questions set out in Exercise 8.1 (see *pp167–8*), whether it is in the past, present or future, you are strengthening the habit of doing so, and taking another small step towards the life that you want.

Ups and downs

It is worth noting, as you move towards freedom from depression, that it will probably not all be plain sailing. For starters, your painful thoughts and feelings are not going to magically disappear. They will probably continue to show up at many points along the way, and that is just fine. It may not be pleasant, and you deserve compassion for the distress that they cause. But so long as you do not allow yourself to react to them in your old, habitual ways, they need be no obstacle to your progress away from depression and towards the life you want.

But there will also be times when old habits take hold of you, and you find yourself lost in thought, struggling with thoughts and feelings, being harsh with yourself, and not doing what matters. This might happen at a particularly stressful or difficult time, or it might happen because things had been going well and so you stopped making an effort to use the skills you have learnt. You might, at times, feel as though you are sliding back into depression.

At these times, remember that this is a normal part of recovery from depression. Everyone finds it hard to resist the pull of old habits, and it is never too late to simply re-engage with your newer, more helpful ones. So, when this happens, there is no need to beat yourself up, to be self-critical, or to despair. When you realise that you have been moving in an unhelpful direction, simply correct course, with an attitude of gentle and kind encouragement.

Exercise 8.2
Getting back on track

Should you find yourself sliding back towards depression, we recommend that you:

■ Take some time to read again about values, in Chapter 7. Remind yourself of what it is that you truly care about and reflect on how close you are to it at the moment.

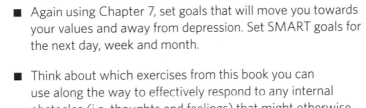

- Again using Chapter 7, set goals that will move you towards your values and away from depression. Set SMART goals for the next day, week and month.

- Think about which exercises from this book you can use along the way to effectively respond to any internal obstacles (i.e. thoughts and feelings) that might otherwise pull you off track. You might decide to practise some exercises more regularly than you have been, and to use particular exercises in particular situations.

- Anticipate any external obstacles that might get in your way, and think about practical ways to deal with them.

- And, once again, be kind to yourself (see Chapter 6) – remember that it is very common for there to be ups as well as downs on the road to a better life.

To help you think through these steps and get back on track, fill in a table like the one on the following page. We have filled it in with an example from Rupert, who we met in Chapters 4 and 7.

What are my values?	What are my goals?	What obstacles might get in my way?	What exercises and practical solutions can I use to deal with the obstacles?	How can I be kind to myself?
Creativity. Sharing what I love.	Today: research music software. This week: buy software and set up home studio. This month: record three of my new songs.	**Internal** Thoughts 'I shouldn't be wasting time like this', 'People would laugh if they knew'. Feelings (Guilt, sadness, shame) **External** The kids are home for the school holidays so we don't have enough space.	**Exercises** Exercise 5.3 The body scan – every morning. Exercise 3.9 I'm having the thought that … – whenever thoughts take control. Exercise 5.5 Turning towards difficulty – whenever feelings take control Exercise 6.4 Pause for compassion – whenever I get a cup of tea. **Practical solutions** Talk to my wife about logistics.	Remind myself that it is natural to find this challenging, and that I'm not the only one who struggles. Reassure myself that I'll be okay and will support myself whatever the outcome. Eat well and exercise, but also take time to relax.

Finally ...

We very much hope that you have found *The Little Depression Workbook* helpful, and that it has inspired you to take the next steps on your journey out of depression. You might do that just by continuing to use the techniques that we have presented here, or by exploring other books or online resources on the third-wave approach (see the *Recommended reading* and *Resources*). Or, better still, you might seek out a therapist to meet with in person – remember that no book can substitute for face-to-face therapy provided by a properly trained professional.

But, however you do it, keep working on whichever skills from this book have been helpful to you, and keep treating yourself kindly as you do so. Remember that your depression is not your fault, and that you are not alone in your suffering. You are more than your depression, and you can move beyond depression towards the life that you want. You can do it, and there is no time like the present.

We wish you well on your journey.

Michael and Michael

Recommended reading

- Gilbert, P., *The Compassionate Mind*. Constable (2010).
- Hanh, T. H., *The Miracle of Mindfulness: The Classic Guide to Meditation by the World's Most Revered Master*. Rider (2008).
- Harris, R., *The I Iappiness Trap: Stop Struggling, Start Living*. Robinson (2008).
- Hayes, S.C., *A Liberated Mind: The Essential Guide to ACT*. Vermilion (2019).
- Hayes, S.C. & Smith, S., *Get out of your Mind and into your Life: The new Acceptance and Commitment Therapy*. New Harbinger (2005).
- Irons, C. & Beaumont, E., *The Compassionate Mind Workbook: A Step-By-Step Guide to Developing Your Compassionate Self*. Robinson (2017).
- Lee-Baggley, D., *Healthy Habits Suck: How to Get Off the Couch and Live a Healthy Life ... Even if You Don't Want To*. New Harbinger Publications (2019).

- Leonard-Curtin, A. & Leonard-Curtin, T., *The Power of Small: How to Make Tiny but Powerful Changes When Everything Feels Too Much*. Hachette Books Ireland (2018).
- Meadows, G., *The Sleep Book: How to Sleep Well Every Night*. Orion (2014).
- Neff, K. & Germer, C. *The Mindful Self-Compassion Workbook: A Proven Way to Accept Yourself, Build Inner Strength, and Thrive*. Guilford Press (2018).
- Oliver, J., Hill, J. & Morris, E., *ACTivate Your Life: Using Acceptance and Mindfulness to Build a Life that is Rich, Fulfilling and Fun*. Robinson (2015).
- Oliver, J. & Bennett, R., *The Mindfulness and Acceptance Workbook for Self-Esteem: Using Acceptance and Commitment Therapy to Move Beyond Negative Self-Talk and Embrace Self-Compassion*. New Harbinger Publications (2020).
- Sinclair, M., Seydel, J. & Shaw, E. *Mindfulness for Busy People: Turning From Frantic and Frazzled into Calm and Composed*. (2nd ed.) Pearson (2017).
- Sinclair, M. & Beadman, M., *The Little ACT Workbook: An Introduction to Acceptance and Commitment Therapy: A Mindfulness-Based Guide for Leading a Full and Meaningful Life*. Crimson (2016).
- Silberstein-Tirch, L.R., *How to Be Nice to Yourself: The Everyday Guide to Self-compassion: Effective Strategies to Increase Self-Love and Acceptance*. Althea Press (2019).

- Strosahl, K.D. & Robinson, P.J., *The Mindfulness and Acceptance Workbook for Depression: Using Acceptance and Commitment Therapy to Move Through Depression and Create a Life Worth Living*. (2nd ed.) New Harbinger (2017).
- Welford, M., *Compassion Focussed Therapy for Dummies*. John Wiley & Sons (2016).
- Williams, M., Teasdale, J., Segal, Z. & Kabat-Zinn, J., *The Mindful Way Through Depression: Freeing Yourself from Chronic Unhappiness*. Guilford Press (2007).

Further resources

Apps (for guided mindfulness practice)

- The ACT Companion: The Happiness Trap App
  www.actcompanion.com
- Headspace
  www.headspace.com
- Buddhify
  www.buddhify.com
- Insight timer
  www.insighttimer.com
- Calm
  www.calm.com

Websites (for resources, workshops, courses and more)

- Association for Contextual Behavioural Science (ACBS)
  www.contextualscience.org
- The Happiness Trap
  www.thehappinesstrap.com

- Act Mindfully
  www.actmindfully.com.au
- The Compassionate Mind Foundation
  www.compassionatemind.co.uk
- Self-Compassion
  www.self-compassion.org
- Centre for Mindfulness Research and Practice
  www.bangor.ac.uk/mindfulness
- Oxford Mindfulness Centre
  www.oxfordmindfulness.org
- Palouse Mindfulness – free online course
  www.palousemindfulness.com

References

- Gilbert, P., *The Compassionate Mind*. Constable (2010).
- Harris, R., *The Happiness Trap: Stop Struggling, Start Living*. Robinson (2008).
- Harris, R., *ACT made simple: An easy-to-read primer on acceptance and commitment therapy* (2nd ed.). Oakland, CA: New Harbinger Publications (2019).
- Hayes, S.C., *A Liberated Mind: The Essential Guide to ACT*. Vermilion (2019).
- Hayes, S.C., Strosahl, K. D. & Wilson, K.G., *Acceptance and commitment therapy: An experiential approach to behavior change*. New York, NY: Guilford Press (1999).
- James, S.L., Abate, D., Abate, K.H., Abay, S.M., Abbafati, C., Abbasi, N. & Murray, C.J.L., 'Global, regional, and national incidence, prevalence, and years lived with disability for 354 diseases and injuries for 195 countries and territories, 1990-2017: A systematic analysis of the Global Burden of Disease Study 2017.' *The Lancet,* 392 (10159), 1789-1858 (2018).
- Neff, K. & Germer, C. *The Mindful Self-Compassion Workbook:*

A Proven Way to Accept Yourself, Build Inner Strength, and Thrive. Guilford Press (2018).

- Polk, K.L., Schoendorff, B., Webster, M. & Olaz, F.O., *The essential guide to the ACT matrix: A step-by-step approach to using the ACT matrix model in clinical practice.* Oakland, CA: New Harbinger Publications (2016).

- Wilson, K.G., Sandoz, E.K., Kitchens, J. & Roberts, M., 'The valued living questionnaire: Defining and measuring valued action within a behavioral framework.' *The Psychological Record*, 60, 249-272 (2010).